D1568053

Lady Gaga

APPLAUSE

To the music lovers in my life:
my parents and my husband, Matt

This edition first published in 2022 by
Palazzo Editions Ltd
15 Church Road
London, SW13 9HE
www.palazzoeditions.com

A CIP catalogue record for this book is available from the British Library.

ISBN 978-1-786750-52-5

Bound and printed in Dubai

10 9 8 7 6 5 4 3 2 1

Designed by Sarah Pyke for Palazzo Editions

ANNIE ZALESKI

Lady Gaga

APPLAUSE

Contents

INTRODUCTION

Previous spread *Lady Gaga performs "La Vie en rose" in Los Angeles, California, on September 30, 2021*

Opposite *Lady Gaga walks onstage to collect her award for International Breakthrough Act at The Brit Awards 2010, held in London, UK, on February 16, 2010*

She intuitively understands what makes pop icons tick: constant creative reinvention, deep self-confidence, and a willingness to be brave.

The history of pop music is driven by bold iconoclasts. In the 1950s, Elvis Presley shook up the establishment with a swivel of his hips and a curl of his lip. A decade later, the clean-cut Beatles induced ecstatic screams with starry-eyed guitar pop and goofy personalities, and then spent the rest of the sixties ripping up the rock 'n' roll rulebook.

David Bowie also became known for his shape-shifting personas, with his evolutions (Ziggy Stardust-era glam drama, the Thin White Duke's austere stance) boasting distinctly theatrical panache. Madonna and Prince dominated the eighties with gusto: The former infused her lithe, worldly dance-pop with frank sexuality and feminist agency, while the latter was a multi-dimensional musical genius fond of ambitious funk-rock seductions and electrified R&B.

And, as the nineties gave way to Y2K and beyond, the girl groups Spice Girls and Destiny's Child—the latter led by future world-changer Beyoncé—and teen-pop icons Britney Spears and Christina Aguilera reconfigured pop once again. Their music was sleek and savvy, driven by equal parts personal empowerment and generous emotional vulnerability, so it was relatable to everyday listeners.

Born Stefani Germanotta on March 28, 1986, Lady Gaga is most certainly a product of these groundbreaking pop epochs. Her stage name is a reference to Queen's 1984 hit "Radio Ga Ga," a song that doubles as an ode to the days when musical greats dominated the airwaves. She's an avowed fan of The Beatles and Bowie—the latter's 1973 LP *Aladdin Sane* is a favorite—and also counts as inspirations acts such as Led Zeppelin, Cyndi Lauper, Bruce Springsteen, and Billy Joel. More importantly, because Gaga grew up learning from these superstars, she intuitively understands what makes pop icons tick: constant creative reinvention, deep self-confidence, and a willingness to be brave.

Not everyone has the fortitude to be this fearless, which is why true pop stars are few and far between. Yet Gaga seemed destined to revolutionize music. She has unicorn-caliber range, and is the rare artist that can nail a heartfelt tribute to *The Sound of Music* at the Oscars; go toe-to-toe with Metallica during a snarling Grammy Awards collaboration; and team up with crooner Tony Bennett, as on 2014's jazz-inflected, Grammy-winning album *Cheek to Cheek*. Like her icon Bowie, she's also comfortable switching up onstage identities when the opportunity arises: In 2010, she assumed the persona of a male character named Jo Calderone for performances.

Gaga has amassed a loyal fanbase because of her open-minded approach to music. Her albums hover around a sonic sweet spot—electro-pop calibrated for marathon dancefloor sessions—but also make room for the occasional power ballad (the piano epic "Speechless"), a twangy rock number ("John Wayne") or rustic country ("Joanne"). Her collaborations, meanwhile, span pop greats (Beyoncé, Ariana Grande), rock gods (Queens of the Stone Age's Josh Homme), and hip-hop stars (T.I.). Even critically-maligned-at-the-time efforts such as 2013's *ARTPOP* have proven to be both influential and beloved—a sign that Gaga is always ahead of the curve.

Opposite *Lady Gaga delivers a tribute to Julie Andrews during the 87th Annual Academy Awards, on February 22, 2015, in Hollywood, California*

Top *Performing "Moth Into Flame" with James Hetfield of Metallica (L) at the 59th Annual Grammy Awards, in Los Angeles, California, on February 12, 2017*

Bottom *July 1, 2014, Montreal, Canada. Lady Gaga surprises the crowd at the Montreal Jazz Festival by joining Tony Bennett (L) onstage.*

Driven and ambitious, New York City-born Gaga started playing piano and writing songs from a very young age, and later took intense acting classes; lead roles in school musicals such as *Guys and Dolls* and *A Funny Thing Happened on the Way to the Forum* soon followed. However, while still a teenager, she also dabbled in more professional endeavors, forming a classic rock cover band and performing during open mic nights held at legendary New York City club The Bitter End. (In a fitting twist, she'd later have a residency there after graduating high school.) Classmates even recall Gaga giving out a demo of original music as a sixteenth birthday party memento.

A stint at New York University's Tisch School of the Arts didn't take, and she dropped out of college by age nineteen. As it turns out, Gaga much preferred the real-world experience she could get in New York City's venues. She went the traditional route at first; vintage footage from this time reveals a passionate songwriter singing her heart out at the piano or enthusiastically fronting what amounts to a bar band. But after a short-lived record deal collapsed, Gaga decided a change was in order. She started doing outrageous cabaret gigs and variety shows, honing a new identity around glam and hard rock sounds and antics—setting hairspray on fire was a favorite move—in grittier Lower East Side clubs.

Her timing (and transformation) was perfect. When Gaga finally landed a record deal that stuck and released 2008's *The Fame*, her presence launched an entirely new pop era. It started, of course, with supersonic dance-pop that drew on the then-red-hot EDM movement ("Just Dance") and older trends such as electroclash ("Beautiful, Dirty, Rich") and punkish disco ("The Fame"). Gaga's voice was as brassy and expressive as a Broadway performer, but she exuded genuine warmth and a cheeky vibe. Who else could sing about wanting to take a spin on someone's "disco stick" with a straight face?

This approach might not seem very original on paper. However, in practice, the way Gaga approached her material gave familiar sounds and themes a glossy makeover. Her fashion was *Jetsons* couture: dramatic makeup, gravity-defying wigs, impractical shoes, space-age costumes. Onstage and in the studio, her innate charisma collided with musical theater-kid quirkiness and long-smoldering ambition; she was the consummate outsider finally crashing the mainstream pop party, doing fancy her own way and dishing out cutting lyrical observations. After years of pop icons maintaining pristine and put-together looks, Gaga was refreshingly weird and unpredictable.

Smartly, Gaga fed off of the delicious tension generated by being a misfit permeating the elite world of celebrity and popularity, as if she were a character in an eighties teen movie. She acknowledged the dark side of celebrity—not for nothing did she title a 2009 expanded reissue of this debut album *The Fame Monster*—but nevertheless embraced the glitzy excess she critiqued. And while other stars might be accused of hypocrisy for such a move, Gaga escaped disapproval by leaning into the utter absurdity of being famous. How else to explain why she wore a disgusting-but-brilliant dress made from raw flank steak at the 2010 MTV Video Music Awards? Or that time she showed up at the Grammy Awards in an egg-shaped cocoon, from which she later emerged to sing "Born This Way"?

Pop music could (and should) be a serious creative endeavor—but Gaga knew pop stardom itself didn't have to be so serious. Yet she also understood that her newfound fame and celebrity could be used for good. Led by the title track, an instant-classic pride anthem that encourages people to be their fully authentic selves, the 2011 album *Born This Way* signaled Gaga's move into advocacy for the LGBTQIA+ community. The following year she and her mother, Cynthia, co-founded the Born This Way Foundation, a youth-oriented nonprofit that remains dedicated to helping promote kindness and mental health. Over the subsequent decade, Gaga would become a philanthropic force, donating significant amounts to Haiti earthquake and Japan tsunami relief, and curating 2020's One World: Together at Home, a benefit concert for the World Health Organization and charities that raised $127 million.

Such empathy also informs her acting forays. While she's portrayed herself on many TV shows (including a memorable turn on *The Simpsons*, as a pop star tasked with helping the depressed residents of Springfield), Gaga has drawn on her theater experience and live musical performances for compelling character work. She won a Golden Globe for her role as the murderous Countess in *American Horror Story: Hotel*, and drew raves for her portrayal of aspiring songwriter Ally Maine in a 2018 remake of *A Star Is Born*. Together, Gaga and her co-star Bradley Cooper had a major hit single with the searing duet "Shallow," which won her another Golden Globe, this time for Best Original Song.

Gaga also stars in the film *House of Gucci*, although her first love remains music. In 2020, months after the pandemic-related lockdown, she released *Chromatica*, a dizzying disco-pop bacchanalia that affirmed her commitment to being open and honest about mental health and wellness. "Rain on Me," her throwback club jam with Ariana Grande, became a massive hit that topped the charts around the world. In a time of great anxiety, when people were forced to stay home, Gaga provided a comforting mood boost.

Where she goes next will be anyone's guess, although what's a little easier to pin down is her legacy. She's set the musical bar high for her pop peers—including Katy Perry, Demi Lovato, and Ellie Goulding—and has been a role model for a new generation of trendsetters: pop wizard Charli XCX, dance floor queens Tove Lo and Dua Lipa, and the genre-blending Olivia Rodrigo.

Pop music is ever-evolving, in a state of perpetual forward motion that's always hurtling toward the future. The artists self-aware enough to realize this fact are better able to survive shifting styles and adapt to changing sonics. Lady Gaga's longevity is a testament not only to her talent, but her open-hearted nature and brilliant foresight.

Simply put, it's her colorful, inclusive planet; we're just lucky enough to be able to visit occasionally and soak up some of her shimmer. Here's how she became the beloved Mother Monster, the patron of nonconforming pop artists everywhere.

Where she goes next will be anyone's guess, although what's a little easier to pin down is her legacy.

Opposite *Lady Gaga as Jo Calderone performs onstage with Brian May (R) at the 28th Annual MTV Video Music Awards on August 28, 2011, in Los Angeles, California*

1

THE BEGINNING

Previous spread *Lady Gaga, 2008*

Opposite *Lady Gaga poses in her origami dress, designed by Glenn Hetrick, 2008*

"When Stefani started to crawl, she would use the leg of the piano to pull herself up and stand, and in doing so, her fingers would eventually land on the keys."
CYNTHIA GERMANOTTA

New York City neighborhoods are crammed full of buildings with interesting architecture and histories. Take the Pythian Temple, located at 135 West 70th Street on the Upper West Side. Built in 1927 as a headquarters and meeting place for the Knights of Pythias, the building boasted Egyptian-inspired details and eventually came to house studio space for Decca Records. In the 1950s, that put the Pythian squarely at the forefront of rock 'n' roll history. Bill Haley & His Comets recorded the seminal single "Rock Around the Clock" during a 1954 session there, while another early rock 'n' roll icon, Buddy Holly, cut what would be his last studio recording at the Pythian in October 1958.

Stefani Joanne Angelina Germanotta, the New York City native who years later became the glamorous jet-setting pop star Lady Gaga, no doubt soaked up some of the Pythian's musical magic after she moved into the building in the early 1990s. (The space had been converted to apartments during the previous decade.) Though barely in elementary school at the time, she was already well on her way to stardom, thanks to a cherished Germanotta family heirloom: a honey-tan piano owned by her parents, Joe and Cynthia Germanotta. Gaga's paternal grandparents originally purchased the humble Everett Piano Co. instrument for $780USD in 1966, and later passed it down to their son and daughter-in-law.

As a toddler, Gaga was mesmerized by the possibilities of this piano. "When Stefani started to crawl, she would use the leg of the piano to pull herself up and stand, and in doing so, her fingers would eventually land on the keys," Cynthia was quoted as saying in news stories about a high-profile 2016 auction for the instrument. "She would stay there and just keep pressing the keys to hear the sound. We would then start to hold her up or sit on the bench and let her tinker."

In an early indication of her singular talent, this tinkering was fruitful. Gaga learned to play the piano by ear—a fact Cynthia discovered after asking her daughter if she wanted lessons. "She was a little bit confused by that because she said that she heard the music in her head," Cynthia later recalled to *InStyle*. "She didn't understand why she had to take a lesson. That was a defining moment because I knew there was something different about her at that point." Gaga confirmed this recollection in a 2008 interview, noting she "hated" lessons at first because playing by ear was "faster ... whereas reading music was more discipline, I had to learn the notes. I hated practicing."

Despite all her grumbling, the practicing had an impact when Gaga was still a young child. Inspired by the cash register sounds at the beginning of Pink Floyd's "Money," the budding composer carefully plotted out and composed her first-ever song called "Dollar Bills" on Mickey Mouse-themed staff paper. "The musical notation was of high quality in comparison to the lyrics on the page—none of which were actually spelled correctly," she later recalled in an early website bio. "I've always had some difficulty saying what I really mean with just words."

In hindsight, all of these achievements foreshadowed Gaga's approach to her eventual career. Although she was given access to resources and support, she didn't wait around for people to teach her about music or art; she manifested her own luck and success by taking charge of her own destiny. Unsurprisingly, Gaga was always uncommonly fearless and commanded attention: The official bio released with *The Fame* mentioned that while dining at tonier Upper West Side restaurants, young Gaga had a penchant for waving breadsticks like a baton while dancing around tables.

Unlike many famous musicians, Gaga didn't have parents who earned a living in the entertainment business. Dad Joe started and later sold a successful company, GuestWiFi, that provided wi-fi to hotels, while Cynthia worked for the telecom giant Verizon. However, Gaga's parents were supportive of their daughter's eccentric behaviors and musical dreams. "[My mom would] tell me, 'Little baby girl, you can be whatever you want, and you are beautiful and you are talented and you could rule the world,'" she later recalled to *Rolling Stone*. To nurture their daughter's talent, Gaga's parents signed her up for piano lessons and also acting classes from the renowned Lee Strasberg Theatre & Film Institute.

From the latter lessons, Gaga learned method acting, an intense style that would later become integral to her music career. "Arguably, it's the most dangerous form of acting, where you embrace becoming the character and you embrace calling upon memory sensory from your life," she said in an interview for the school's website. "It's powerful and it takes you back implicitly to a place that you remember as a child. It's very strong."

In addition to encouraging her to pursue the arts, the Germanottas also prioritized education. Gaga and her younger sister, Natali, attended Convent of the Sacred Heart, an all-girls Catholic school with rigorous academics and famous attendees such as Caroline Kennedy, Gloria Morgan Vanderbilt, and Nicky Hilton. Although Sacred Heart had an excellent reputation and was considered prestigious, the student body itself was diverse. "There were lots of different kinds of girls," Gaga told *New York*.

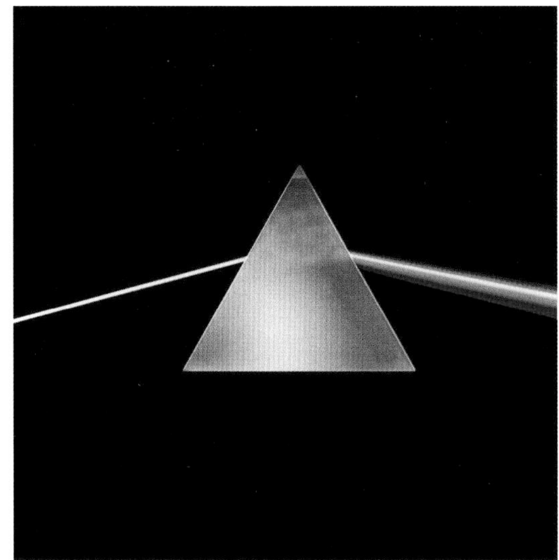

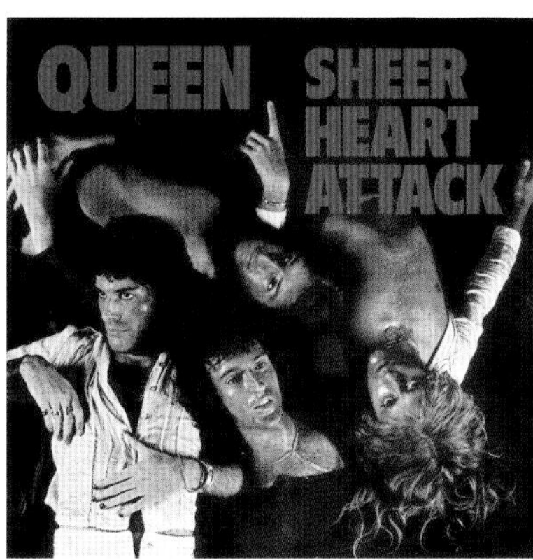

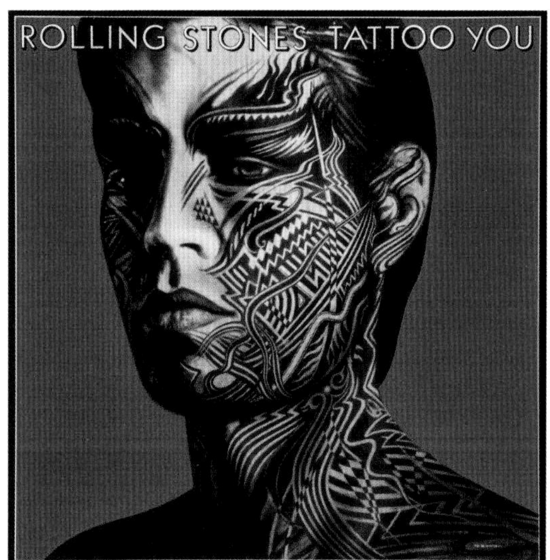

Opposite *Cynthia and Joseph Germanotta, Lady Gaga's parents, pictured on February 16, 2010, in New York City*

Album covers clockwise from top left *Dark Side of The Moon, Pink Floyd, 1973; Tattoo You, Rolling Stones, 1981; Sheer Heart Attack, Queen, 1974. Classic rock artists played in heavy rotation at Gaga's family home, and had a formative influence on her.*

"Some had extreme wealth, others were on welfare and scholarship, and some were in the middle, which was my family. All our money went into education and the house."

By all accounts, Gaga's home life was happy—and provided her with a foundational musical education. Thanks to her New Jersey native dad, a major classic rock aficionado, she became a huge fan of icons with striking visual presences and personal charisma. On the family's living room record player, he spun albums by Billy Joel, Pink Floyd, The Rolling Stones, Queen, David Bowie, and Led Zeppelin. Gaga also became a massive fan of The Beatles, and later got a tattoo of a peace sign on her left wrist in honor of the city's *Imagine* memorial to John Lennon. And, in a nod to the family's Italian-American heritage, opera superstar Andrea Bocelli and Frank Sinatra's *Duets* were also in heavy rotation. "[My dad] used to pick me up when I was a kid and he would twirl me around," she recalled in an early 2008 interview about her formative musical years and listening sessions. "I had a really amazing childhood: a lot of culture, a lot of meatballs, a lot of marinara."

Rocker Bruce Springsteen was an even bigger touchstone for young Gaga—in no small part because her dad, who once played in bands on the Jersey Shore, was also a big fan. Not only did she soak up lyrical and thematic inspiration from "The Boss", but his music also inadvertently helped her advance in her career. One Christmas, the teenaged Gaga received a Springsteen songbook for the piano that included her favorite song, "Thunder Road," the lead track from 1975 album *Born to Run*. "My dad said, 'If you learn how to play this song, we will take out a loan for a grand

piano, a baby grand,'" she said in the MTV documentary *Lady Gaga: Inside the Outside*. "I didn't know the difference." By this time, Gaga had been taking piano lessons for years, and so learning "Thunder Road" was a challenge, since it was so different from the classical pieces she was used to performing. "I was playing these huge pieces, like 15 pages long ... and then there was this Bruce Springsteen song," she continued. "I opened up the book and there was, like, guitar chords. I was so confused; I didn't understand it, so I just started to read it and eventually, eventually I got it down."

Gaga paired her classic rock grounding with a love of flashy pop icons, and would listen to eighties superstars Cyndi Lauper and Michael Jackson on her tape player. She also gravitated toward strong women, such as nineties alt-rock group Garbage—a band fronted by Scottish firebrand Shirley Manson—and NYC avant-garde punks Blondie. "When I was in middle school, I had a rotation of your albums and Garbage's albums," she told Blondie frontwoman, Debbie Harry, during a *Harper's Bazaar* interview. "I used to put them in my Discman and walk around the block because my mom wouldn't let me walk more than one block by myself." Blondie in particular can be seen as an early blueprint for Gaga's career. The band were music video innovators—in fact, they filmed clips for every song on 1979's *Eat to the Beat*, creating a video album long before it was a common method of promotion—and Harry was an influential fashion icon who embraced both DIY punk couture and high-fashion sophistication.

However, Gaga was also very much a child of the nineties MTV generation. During the height of the teen-pop movement driven by *NSYNC and Britney Spears, she and friends would head for Times Square after school, and stand in the crowd outside of MTV's offices while *Total Request Live* was filming, in the hopes of catching a glimpse of the day's guest stars. In a prescient example of foreshadowing, the MTV Video Music Awards were also must-see TV for a young Gaga. As a teen who loved pop music, she was drawn especially to the awards held in 2001, which featured Alicia Keys performing "Fallin'" and Michael Jackson guesting with *NSYNC for their hit "Pop."

By the time she hit adolescence, Gaga had also amassed plenty of experience honing an offbeat fashion sense. In kindergarten, she went the DIY route for her costume when she acted in *Three Billy Goats Gruff*, fashioning billy goat horns "out of tinfoil and a hanger," she told *The Guardian*. Gaga also pretended to dress up when watching the MTV Video Music Awards by draping a cozy, hand-knitted afghan around her body and imagining it was fancy formalwear. Perhaps even more important, she learned that being fashionable involved hard work and sacrifice: In high school, she took a job as a waitress in a diner; one of her first splurges after starting to get paid was a Gucci purse. "I was so excited because all the girls at Sacred Heart always had their fancy purses, and I always had whatever," she told *New York*. "My mom and dad were not buying me a $600 purse."

When Gaga reached high school, her career ambitions started to crystallize. At age fourteen, she connected with Don Lawrence, a voice teacher who counted celebs such as Christina Aguilera, U2's Bono, and Mick Jagger as clients. As with many things in her career, meeting Lawrence happened due to a combination of luck and happenstance. She was singing a Backstreet Boys song to herself in a store near her house, and was stopped by the owner, who was a musician. "[He] pulled me aside and slipped a phone number in my hand," she recalled in an early bio. "He told me his uncle was a highly respected voice teacher who he thought would like to work with me." That uncle just so happened to be Lawrence.

Opposite *The peace tattoo visible on Lady Gaga's left wrist is in honor of John Lennon*

Left *With Bruce Springsteen (R)—another music hero of Gaga's—during a concert to celebrate the Rainforest Fund's 21st birthday at Carnegie Hall on May 13, 2010, in New York City*

Blondie (left) and nineties rock band Garbage (right, 1995)—bands both fronted by strong women—were early blueprints for Gaga

"When I was in middle school, I had a rotation of your albums and Garbage's albums. I used to put them in my Discman and walk around the block because my mom wouldn't let me walk more than one block by myself."

LADY GAGA TO DEBBIE HARRY

As a high school freshman, she also formed and fronted a classic rock cover band that favored songs by Led Zeppelin, U2, Pink Floyd, and Jefferson Airplane; this nascent group frequented local open-mic nights. Gaga's mom also accompanied her to New York City clubs, where the aspiring talent honed her solo act. "These were jazz bars not sex clubs," Gaga later told *The Independent*. "They would have open mic nights so my mother would take me along and say, 'My daughter's very young but she's very talented. I'll sit with her as she plays.'"

This vocal training and live experience boosted her confidence and made her unafraid to take risks, but also gave her a reputation for versatility. Gaga became known as a performer who could sing anything. For example, casting directors for a high school production of *A Funny Thing Happened on the Way to the Forum* persuaded her to play a challenging soprano role, Philia, even though her vocal sweet spot was usually as an alto. "She knew it wasn't her bread and butter, but she just forged on and did the best she could," James Phillips, who taught music at Regis High School, Sacred Heart's brother school, told TODAY. "She knew it would take a little extra work and she was not adverse to that."

Despite her prodigious (and precocious) talent, Gaga was also a normal, quasi-rebellious teenager. "I was a bad kid," she later recalled to *Rolling Stone*. "So I had a lot of home issues when I was in high school especially. I was a fucking nightmare." She dated an older man, had a fake I.D., and would party downtown on weekends. Teachers also chided her for wearing low-cut shirts that revealed too much cleavage. However, some of her renegade moves, such as a tattoo of a G-clef on her lower back, were very in character. "Before I made my first big music video, I decided to turn that tattoo into a huge side piece," she later told *New York*. "I just couldn't face the world with a tramp stamp." As that tattoo implies, this wild child behavior didn't dampen her ambition. "She was always extremely driven, extremely hardworking," her mom said in *The Daily Beast*. "If she had to go to a voice lesson and her friends wanted to hang out, they wouldn't always understand. With her, it was a passion. Not a hobby."

But like many artistic, ambitious and talented kids, Gaga suffered due to her single-minded devotion to the performing arts. "Let's say that she was uniquely very different growing up and her peers didn't always appreciate that," her mom diplomatically told *InStyle* years later. "As a result, she experienced some meanness and cruelty at various

Left *Performing at the Sap Arena in Mannheim, Germany, on August 29, 2008*

times—things like being taunted, isolated, humiliated, both in school and out of school." A classmate later recalled that older girls mocked Gaga in secret ("They always talked behind her back, like, 'Gross, she's the Germ! She's dirty!'"), while Gaga herself says she was also teased for her looks: having a big nose, an intense self-tan, and a penchant for sculpting dramatic eyebrows. "I used to do these really big Evita brows," she told *Rolling Stone*.

Not everyone remembers Gaga as being a misfit, however. "She was always popular," Julia Lindenthal, who attended a nearby high school, told *New York*. "I don't remember her experiencing any social problems or awkwardness." (Gaga didn't name names, but in a 2011 *Rolling Stone* interview, she refuted quotes from former classmates talking up her popularity: "I've seen all of those quotes, and all of those people were bullies! Perhaps it's their way of trying to redeem themselves.") Regis High School's James Phillips, however, also remembered a memorable high school play where a supportive crowd was losing their minds cheering and screaming in reaction to Gaga's performance because it was so good. "It wasn't something she tried to incite," he added. "Even though it wasn't her own songs, everyone recognized that she was talented and exceptional even for a high-school kid."

And if some of her peers begrudged her talent, others recognized that she was going places. When Gaga held a sixteenth birthday bash, attendees received a demo featuring some of her original songs as a parting gift. It made quite an impression. "Everyone was playing her demo, like, 'Whoa, she's going to be a star,'" Justin Rodriguez, a Regis High School graduate, told *New York*. "She was by far the most talented person in high school, but she'd do so many random acts of kindness, like saying, 'Your singing has gotten so much better, you're working hard and I've noticed.' She wasn't a diva at all."

Despite her early achievements, Gaga had a long way to go before she attained the stardom she so craved. Little did she know then, what a wild and unexpected path her life would take.

2

BECOMING GAGA

Previous spread *Lady Gaga performs in front of a sold out crowd at the Susquehanna Bank Center on December 14, 2008, Camden, New Jersey, USA*

Opposite *Lady Gaga with performers at the Open A.I.R. Summer Concert Series in New York on May 15, 2008*

Stefani Germanotta didn't just snap her fingers one day and transform into Lady Gaga. Although she spent her formative years working toward a career in music and performing, ascending into global pop stardom took time, effort and extensive trial-and-error. She suffered setbacks along the way, although her deep resiliency and intense ambition served as protective shields of sorts against potentially fatal career blows.

First, however, Gaga embraced one of the biggest teenage rite of passages: going to college. Like many driven high school students, Gaga couldn't wait to head off into the real world. In fact, at age seventeen, she was one of twenty students picked for the prestigious musical theater conservatory called the Collaborative Arts Project 21 (CAP21), which was then affiliated with New York University's Tisch School of the Arts. She entered the program during the 2004–2005 school year, where she studied art history and music—and quickly made an impression on the faculty there.

"It was so clear that she knew what she was doing," Christine Dhimos, the dance chair at CAP21 who was Gaga's ballet teacher and advisor, told TODAY. "It wasn't that she was some flaky person living in la-la land. Somebody like that you want to encourage to follow what they want to pursue."

"It was so clear that she knew what she was doing. It wasn't that she was some flaky person living in la-la land."
CHRISTINE DHIMOS

Gaga was indeed very serious about her art. In March 2005, she performed two original songs at an NYU cancer benefit, UltraViolet Live. Sporting a strapless green top and a long white skirt, she displayed intense concentration while playing and singing at the piano. The first song, "Captivated," was an earnest love song ballad; her second choice, "Electric Kiss," was brisker and more dramatic, with lyrics such as "I'm gonna change the world with my lips" and Gaga pounding on the keys forcefully. She ended up placing third overall at the event.

Left *New York University's Tisch School of the Arts, where Gaga studied music and art history from 2004-2005*

Opposite *Nada Surf, 2003. Gaga opened for the pop-rock band in the early days of her career.*

As a video of the benefit shows, college freshman Gaga wasn't yet an out-of-this-world pop star. "She was a very suburban, preppy, friendly, social party girl," an ex-dorm-mate anonymously told the *New York Post* in 2010. "There was nothing that would tip you off that she had this Warhol-esque, 'new art' extremism." According to another unnamed source, Gaga's then-version of having a "crazy" outfit was "putting suspenders on her jeans."

But even if her fashion sense hadn't yet developed its edge, her ambition was already in full bloom. In April, Gaga performed a solo acoustic set opening for the pop-rock band Nada Surf at the South Street Seaport. A month later, she did two shows in a week at legendary New York clubs: a May 26 gig at the punk dive CBGB, and a June 1 show at the Lower East Side club Pianos. By this time, the school year was over, and she had turned her attention to playing out as much as she could.

The summer after her freshman year of college was pivotal for her musical development. Gaga rented an apartment at Stanton and Clinton on the Lower East Side and started pursuing gigs at New York City music venues. She recalls finagling bookings using every trick in the book, including little white lies and subterfuge. "I remember once pretending to be my own PR rep, calling to book 'STEFANI, an emerging talent,' and booked myself later in the week," stated an old bio. Paul Colby and Kenny Gorka, who co-owned Greenwich Village club The Bitter End, saw Gaga's talent even without her sleight of hand; in fact, the club became something of a second home for her, and she regularly performed there. "She was learning how to put on a show," Gorka told the *New York Daily News*. "She learned to get people to listen."

At this point, Gaga's music was quite different—"bittersweet rock ballads to power-pop rock," as she put it in her early bio. This range helped her land some rather unique gigs. On September 3, 2005, Gaga performed at an NYU-affiliated Hurricane Relief Show + Downtown Welcome Event at the South Street Seaport. On October 10, she performed the original song "No Floods" at the sixtieth Annual Columbus Day Parade in New York City, where she drew praise from one of the TV journalists: "Wow, what a voice!" he exclaimed. By this time, school had lost its allure: In fall 2005, she decided to take time off from NYU and focus on her music career. "I hated it," she said in 2008, of going to college. "Not the studying—I was a good student, I love to learn. But I wanted to work, and I wanted to make music."

Her parents weren't necessarily thrilled, but they supported her decision, with one condition: She had a hard deadline of one year to make things happen and land a record deal. Gaga quickly got to work. Within weeks of leaving NYU, she put together The Stefani Germanotta Band (sometimes called SGBand) with bassist Eli Silverman, drummer Alex Beckmann and guitarist Calvin Pia. The

group had a "really dingy practice space" that was "under some grocery store, where you'd have to enter through those metal doors on the sidewalk," Pia told *The New York Observer*. Back then, Gaga herself "was very bubbly, very eccentric, very driven," he added, noting she'd drag her gigantic keyboard to the space from her nearby apartment. "The high art thing? I did not see any hints of that!"

In October 2005, Gaga and the full-band debuted at The Bitter End, and continued to perform around New York City venues such as the Knitting Factory and The Lion's Den. Unsurprisingly, The Stefani Germanotta Band's style wasn't a far cry from Gaga's solo work. Vintage footage of the group performing Led Zeppelin's "D'yer Mak'er" at the Bitter End in early 2006 is laid-back and jammy. Gaga sounds soulful, but channels her inner Robert Plant as the song progresses.

A five-song demo called the *Words* EP also captures the band's sound during this period. The tunes are well-wrought and catchy, but aren't necessarily easy to pick out as Gaga songs. While her vocal power is evident, the musical style is all over the map, encompassing mid-tempo piano ballads ("Wish You Were Here," not the Pink Floyd song), Broadway-esque ("Something Crazy") and funky blues-rock ("No Floods"). That EP was followed in March 2006 by another EP, *Red and Blue*.

In April 2006, Gaga played a solo show at Sin-é, a legendary venue that helped boost the careers of artists such as Jeff Buckley, Sinéad O'Connor, and The Waterboys. Gaga also collaborated with hip-hop icon Melle Mel from Grandmaster Flash and the Furious Five and recorded two songs, "World Family Tree" and "The Fountain of Truth," for the audio CD paired with *The Portal in the Park*, a children's book by the author Cricket Casey.

Her hard work and constant gigging paid dividends. In spring 2006, she started working with the New Jersey producer Rob Fusari, who co-wrote Destiny's Child's "No, No, No" and also co-produced the trio's "Bootylicious" as well as Will Smith's "Wild Wild West." The two met purely by chance, via an artist by the name of Wendy Starland, who happened to be part of a songwriters showcase at the Cutting Room that also featured Gaga. Starland was impressed by the headliner's poise and vocal prowess. "Her presence is enormous," she told *New York*. "And fearless. I listened for the pitch, the tone, and timbre of her voice. Was she able to have a huge dynamic range? Was she able to get soft and then belt? And I felt that she was able to do all that while giving out this very powerful energy."

"I hated it. Not the studying–I was a good student, I love to learn. But I wanted to work, and I wanted to make music." LADY GAGA

As it turns out, Starland was already working with Fusari, and he had given her a quest: Find him a female artist that could be the figurehead of a rock band like the Strokes. Gaga didn't necessarily fit the bill; in fact, she wasn't even necessarily in the same ballpark. Fusari told *New York* his first impression was that she was "a Guidette, totally *Jersey Shore*" and he actually felt bad she had taken a forty-minute bus ride from the city to his studio in Parsippany, New Jersey. "I'm thinking, 'How can I cut this short and still make her feel like it was worth coming all the way out here?'" he told the *New York Daily News*. "She was bubbly and nice, but not what I was looking for at all."

However, Gaga's charisma and flair were undeniable, and she convinced him to open his mind and embrace a different kind of New York talent. "She didn't have that kind of under-singing character voice of Julian Casablancas, so I dropped the Strokes thing right away," Fusari told *New York*. "I thought she was a female John Lennon, to be totally honest. She was the oddest talent."

Gaga and her dad teamed up with Fusari to form a company, Team Love Child, to handle her music career development. From there, she started diligently commuting from New York City to Fusari's studio in Parsippany, New Jersey. They'd work together seven days a week, with lunch breaks at the chain restaurant Chili's to regroup and recharge. Together, the musician and producer started making "a very heavy rock record ... hard and grungy," he told *Billboard*. However, the direction wasn't quite jelling—until Fusari saw what Nelly Furtado had done to turn her career fortunes around: Evolve from doing hip-hop-tinged folk songs such as 2000's "I'm Like a Bird" to sleeker, beat-heavy tunes such as "Promiscuous" with Timbaland.

"My antenna went up," Fusari explained to *Billboard*. "I said, 'Stef, take a look at this. I'm really an R&B guy. I never produced a rock record in my life. I don't know, you think maybe we should shift gears?'" He recalled she was reluctant at first and protested the change, but his persuasive arguments won out. "I'm like, 'Stef, just try

Left *New York's legendary Greenwich Village club, The Bitter End, where Gaga honed her live performances*

Left *Hip-hop icon Melle Mel with Grandmaster Flash and the Furious Five. In early 2006, Gaga collaborated with Mel on two songs for an audio CD to accompany* The Portal in the Park, *a children's book by Cricket Casey.*

this. Let's at least abandon the live drums and some of the guitars.' I finally got her to agree, and that day we did 'Beautiful, Dirty, Rich,' which was me sitting at an MPC drum machine and Stef playing her piano riff."

"Beautiful, Dirty, Rich" is a far cry from her solo piano work: Its neon-hued pop vibe sounds fresh, a collision of mainstream sass and edgy New York City dance grooves. Gaga would later claim in a June 2008 interview she "was doing a lot of drugs" when she wrote the song, although you can already pinpoint the themes she'd explore *The Fame* coming together very coherently. "Whoever you are or where you live, you can self-proclaim this inner fame based on your personal style, and your opinions about art and the world, despite being conscious of it," she said, and noted the song also critiqued Lower East Side poseurs. "There was a lot of rich kids who did drugs and said that they were poor artists, so it's also a knock at that." She mimicked one of these kids ("Daddy I'm so sorry, I'm so, so sorry, yes / We just like to party") and then added, "I used to hear my friends on the phone with their parents, asking for money before they would go buy drugs. That was an interesting time for me."

Together, Fusari and Gaga continued working up songs. Perhaps even more important, it was in this period that Stefani Germanotta started going by Lady Gaga. As might be expected, the origin stories vary for her name and persona. In one version, the moniker was said to be inspired by a nickname derived from Queen's 1984 hit "Radio Ga Ga." In another telling, Fusari sang "Radio Ga Ga" to her in the studio—and when he attempted to text her the song's title, his phone's auto-correct somehow changed it to "Lady Gaga," and she ran with it. To muddy the waters further, the *New York Post* claimed in 2010 the name "Lady Gaga" developed in a marketing meeting.

At any rate, Gaga's music and presence were finally starting to attract attention from record labels. Fusari slipped her demo to Island Def Jam, which called Gaga in for an audition. Joshua Sarubin, who worked in A&R for the

> **"I didn't want to start singing while they were talking, so I got undressed. That's when I made a real decision about the kind of pop artist that I wanted to be. Because it was a performance art moment there and then."** LADY GAGA

label, told *NJ.com* he remembered her as being "unusual," perhaps because she oozed self-assurance. "She sat down at the piano in a showcase room and the way she played and the lyrics and the way she acted and sang was just so different and in your face, and you couldn't turn away. She was wearing these crazy white thigh-high boots and a black minidress and she had this presence like, 'I'm sexy and I don't care what anybody has to say about it.'"

Fusari recalls then-label head Antonio "L.A." Reid also being bowled over during the audition as she played an early composition called "Wonderful." "I guess they have some system that when somebody's really good, L.A. gets a secret bat signal to come in. So he enters as she's playing and by the end he's enamored. He looks at her and says, 'Before you leave the building, you have to stop down in legal and sign my contract.'" Reid himself later told *Access Hollywood* he recalled a similar lightning-bolt moment during this Gaga performance. "When she was done, I said, 'You are an amazing artist, a true star, and you will change music,' and I signed her."

The record deal with Island Def Jam didn't happen right away, as Gaga smartly weighed other options before signing on the dotted line. However, the label seemed like a good home—at the time, their roster also included acts like Rihanna and Ne-Yo—and she signed a contract. Unfortunately, the honeymoon period ended up being short-lived, as Gaga's tenure on the label was distinguished not by demo time or development help, but by Reid's disinterest. "He wouldn't give her the time of day," Fusari recalled to *Billboard*. "She'd want to sit in a room with him and talk about her music, and he just wouldn't do it. We still don't know why." Reid also allegedly wasn't impressed with the recorded demos he heard several months later. With little fanfare, Island Def Jam dropped her.

After she became a star, Reid later admitted he regretted his decision, blaming his change of heart on the fact he was "having a bad day" and telling *Access Hollywood* that cutting her loose "was the worst thing I've ever done." However, the damage was done, and a devastated Gaga retreated to New York City to lick her wounds, smarting at the thought her chance at stardom had disappeared. "I went back to my apartment on the Lower East Side, and I was so depressed," she told *New York*. "That's when I started the real devotion to my music and art."

In hindsight, this post-record deal period was both the wildest and most transformative time of Gaga's life. In photos taken in the 2006–2008 era, you can trace her evolution from an ambitious piano-rock prodigy to a no-holds-barred glam-rock 'n' roller. This reinvention also illustrated her resilience. Despite the massive setback of a lost record deal, she poured her heart and soul into music and creativity—and pushed herself to embrace the kind of fearlessness needed for pop stardom. "I used to take my demo into clubs," she told *Rolling Stone*, "but I would lie and say that I was Lady Gaga's manager, and that she was only available to play on Friday nights at 10.30pm—the best time slot." Speaking to *The Independent* in 2009, Gaga also recalled a particularly rough performance where the crowd was chatty and rude. Fueled by "a couple of drinks," and fired up by her new songs and an "amazing outfit," she all but demanded they pay attention to her.

"I sat down, cleared my throat and waited for everyone to go quiet. It was a bunch of frat kids from the West Village and I couldn't get them to shut up. I didn't want to start singing while they were talking, so I got undressed. There I was sitting at the piano in my underwear. So they shut up." Gaga added that this snap decision to disrobe was a turning point: "That's when I made a real decision about the kind of pop artist that I wanted to be. Because it was a performance art moment there and then."

Opposite *Lollapalooza, August 4, 2007, in Chicago, Illinois*

Glam icons such as T.Rex (above) and Cockney Rebel (opposite) had a profound impact on Gaga's evolution as an artist

Gaga also started go-go dancing at New York City's dive bars, which were dominated by "a lot of nerdy, record-collecting DJs" and club kids, she said in an early 2008 interview. "People have personas; the nightclubs feel like a culture. The music is underground, but it's also mainstream." Her musical taste also expanded during this time: She became heavily into glam, especially genre icons such as T. Rex and Cockney Rebel ("It's a sub-set of all these things I love: cabaret, burlesque, metal, rock," she told *The Guardian*) and also rekindled her long-standing love of Queen and David Bowie.

The latter's 1973 LP *Aladdin Sane* was a heavy-rotation favorite. "I'd open the window so my neighbors could hear it up the fire escape, and I'd sit out on the ledge, have a cigarette and listen," she told *The Guardian*, and then called out Bowie's vocals on "Watch That Man" specifically while adding, "I like to think I sing like a man. I want people to feel invaded when I sing. It's very confrontational." She also became "fascinated with Eighties club culture," she told *Rolling Stone*, as well as more cutting-edge alternative acts: gloomy post-punk band the Cure, synth-pop icons Pet Shop Boys and modern electro-pop act the Scissor Sisters.

All of these inspirations had a profound impact on her evolution as an artist and the music she was starting to explore. "When I was playing the New York rock clubs, a lot of record labels thought I was too theatrical," she told *The Daily Mail*. "Then when I auditioned for stage musicals, the producers said I was too pop."

However, during this period, her friendship group also expanded exponentially. She started hanging out with Justin Tranter, who fronted the glam-kissed rock band Semi Precious Weapons and would later become a successful pop songwriter. The pair would go shopping together, Tranter later recalled to *New York*: "Any sex store where 99 percent of the store was made up of DVDs and sex toys and 1 percent was actual clothing was our favorite place to shop. Her mom came to my loft once to pick up one Lucite pump that she left at the show the night before." Gaga also started dating Lüc Carl, the manager of the Lower East Side dive bar St. Jerome's, who drove a green Camino and was once described as having "loud Nikki Sixx hair." The pair would be in each other's lives on and off for years, and Carl would inspire Gaga songs all the way through 2011's *Born This Way*.

At St. Jerome's, Gaga also met and befriended a performance artist/go-go dancer named Lady Starlight, a fan of glam and heavy metal who became a formative influence. "I'll never forget when she turned to me one day

and she said, 'You're a performance artist,'" Gaga told *Rolling Stone*. "I was like, 'You think so?' When people believe in you, that's what makes you grow." For Gaga, this support system arrived at the perfect time, as she was exploring new sounds, new identities, new fashions. "They gave me a sense of belonging somewhere," she confessed to *Rolling Stone*. "It'll make me cry just talking about it, because when you feel so much like you don't fit in anywhere, you'd do anything just to make a fucking friend. And when I met the right people, they really supported me."

Lady Starlight served as a mentor of sorts to Gaga, including inviting her to a dance party called Frock N Roll, because she "wanted to bring [Gaga] into my world," as she put it to *The New York Post*. Not everybody was immediately welcoming, Starlight noted: "You know how it is in those kinds of artsy circles. People are a little snooty." This reluctance might have come from the fact Gaga was still trying to come into her own as capital-G Gaga. "She was wearing a version of [the eventual look]," Starlight says. "Definitely spandex, for sure, some kind of unitard, but casual. She still looked abrupt and out of place."

Creatively, the women also put together a wild, raunchy variety show. "The very first show we did was kind of the best show ever," Lady Starlight later told *TODAY*. "There was all these singer/songwriter girls like Alanis Morissette and Norah Jones. And we were all turntables, keyboards and bikinis. The tourists were staring full on." The duo became known for setting hairspray on fire during a revue that also drew on burlesque, electroclash and other out-there performance art moves.

At this point, Gaga's fashion sense was heavily influenced by what was going on around her in the Lower East Side. During a candid 2008 interview, she characterized the approach as "rock star's girlfriend": "It was not so much, 'I want to be the greatest rock 'n' roll band that ever lived'—I wanted to be the greatest rock 'n' roll band that ever lived lead singer's girlfriend. I wanted to be the girl backstage at the Mötley Crüe concert in the feather dress doing Nikki Sixx's eyeliner."

Gaga also started making her own outfits because it was more affordable, mixing and matching fabrics such as leather and sequins, even as she admired the luxe style and cuts of fashion greats: Fendi, Versace, Gucci, Dolce & Gabbana. As she mused in 2008, the mix of low-brow culture and high fashion posed a challenge: "How do you make five dollars look like five grand? How do you feel like five grand when you've got five bucks in your pocket?"

Fusari was less than impressed when he saw Gaga's revue with Lady Starlight, telling *New York*, "It was *Rocky Horror* meets eighties band, and I didn't get it at all. I told Stefani that I could get her another DJ, but she was like, 'I'm good.'" Gaga's father also wasn't necessarily thrilled to see his daughter onstage in outfits such as a leopard-print G-string and a black tank top. "He thought I was crazy," she told *Rolling Stone*. "It wasn't 'She's inappropriate' or 'She's a bad girl' or 'She's a slut.' He thought I was nuts, that I was doing drugs and had lost my mind and had no concept of reality anymore. For my father, it was an issue of sanity."

Admittedly, he may have had reason to worry, as Gaga later confessed she was partying and overindulging during this period. To *Rolling Stone* journalist Neil Strauss, she revealed her apartment had bedbugs and roaches, as well as "mirrors with cocaine everywhere. [I had] no will or interest in doing anything but making music and getting high." In a separate *Rolling Stone* interview, she stressed her parents and childhood had nothing to do with her debauched behavior; instead, she was emulating some of her heroes. "All of the things I went through were on my own quest for an artistic journey to fuck myself up like Warhol and Bowie and Mick, and just go for it. All of the trauma I caused to myself. Or it was caused by people that I met when being outrageous and irresponsible."

Still, Gaga's drive never wavered. In August 2007, she performed an early morning set at the major music festival

Lollapaloooza. In hindsight, the performance is charming: The crowd looks like they have *no idea* what to make of Gaga, who struts her stuff in front of the stage through disco-punk jams "Dirty Ice Cream" and "Disco Heaven" and steps behind a keyboard for more introspective moments. Her outfit was also delightfully oddball: She sported a disco ball bra—"My boobs look like two disco balls [in the bra]," she told an early interviewer—high stockings and skimpy underwear.

Despite his skepticism about her new direction, Fusari still believed in Gaga. He connected her with his frequent producer collaborator, Vincent Herbert, who had worked with R&B stars Destiny's Child and Toni Braxton and had a label imprint, Streamline Records, with ties to Interscope Records. With the blessing of the latter's Jimmy Iovine, Herbert signed Gaga, giving her a second chance at major label stardom.

Thanks to this deal, Gaga started co-writing songs for other pop artists, including New Kids on the Block ("Full Service"), the Pussycat Dolls ("Elevator"), Britney Spears ("Quicksand") and others. "I don't have an ego about other people singing my songs," she said in a 2009 *Billboard* cover story. As it turns out, this songwriting work helped connect the dots for her initial career success. She crossed

At Lower East Side dive bar St. Jerome's, Gaga met DJ Lady Starlight (above, left) who became something of a mentor to Gaga and Lüc Carl (above, right) with whom she would be in an on-again-off-again relationship for a number of years.

paths with rapper Akon, who was working with a producer called RedOne. Akon was duly impressed by her vocal and songwriting skills. "When I see a star, I just know it," he recalled to *Entertainment Weekly* in 2018. "From the moment she walked in [for our first meeting], her appearance and her attitude felt brand new and fresh. She was so fearless."

Akon signed Gaga to his label, KonLive, and they dug in and started working on music. In spring 2008, the world heard their first official music from Lady Gaga: "Just Dance." Co-written with RedOne, who also produced the song, "Just Dance" came together in just ten minutes in the studio. Although the song was almost given to the Pussycat Dolls, Gaga recorded it herself, and the rest is history.

Gaga was officially on her way—although, as she noted pointedly in a 2009 *Rolling Stone* cover story, she'd "always been Gaga" all along. "It's just that all the years of schooling and being in a Catholic environment and living in a place where we were kind of told what was the right way to be, I suppressed all those eccentricities about myself so I could fit in.

"Once I was free, I was able to be myself," she added. "I pulled her out of me, and I found that all of the things about myself that I so desperately tried to suppress for so many years were the very things that all my art and music friends thought were so lovely about me, so I embraced them."

Above *Lady Gaga (far right) walks onstage at the Slipper Room in New York, 2007, where she and Lady Starlight performed The New York Street Revival and Trash Dance—a wild, raunchy variety show*

Right *Justin Tranter (L) of Semi Precious Weapons, another main player in Gaga's influential and growing circle of friends*

JUST DANCE

Previous spread *Lady Gaga performs onstage during Z100's Jingle Ball 2008 at Madison Square Garden on December 12, 2008, in New York City*

Opposite *Onstage at the Q102 Jingle Ball, on December 14, 2008, in Camden, New Jersey, USA*

"I just felt so free, and there was nothing in my way." LADY GAGA

Artists face enormous stress when they sign a record deal, including label deadlines, creative expectations and self-imposed pressure. However, Lady Gaga seemed remarkably chill when she started working on the music that would end up on her debut album, *The Fame*. In January 2008, she spent a productive week in California at the famed Record Plant with co-collaborator RedOne, polishing off what would become three of her biggest hits: "Just Dance," "Poker Face," and "LoveGame."

"I just felt so free," she later recalled to *Rolling Stone*, "and there was nothing in my way."

The Fame's sound reflects this freedom. In addition to all the synth-stacked dance music, the album encompasses new wave ("I Like It Rough"), disco-pop ("The Fame"), electro-soul ("Starstruck"), and hip-hop ("Paper Gangsta"). There's even a piano ballad, "Brown Eyes," that doesn't feel far removed from the music she was doing in college. *The Fame*'s inspirations were similarly eclectic, and encompassed both her formative years and artistic evolution. "My music is pretty much a reflection of my transition from New York uptown to New York downtown, and all the things that I've discovered," she said in a 2008 video interview.

Gaga told *The Guardian* she was listening to The Beatles' *Abbey Road* when writing *The Fame*, noting the LP's "sense of melody in conjunction with very liberating, strange storytelling, and it's a complete body of work from beginning to end." However, the way she described *The Fame* to MTV UK seemed more like The Beatles' *The White Album*: "This record is really different. You've got club bangers to more 70s Glam to more singer-songwriter records to rock music. *The Fame* is not about who you are—it's about how everybody wants to know who you are."

The latter statement certainly reflects Gaga's not-so-secret desire to be known by everyone the world over.

Opposite *Lady Gaga*, 2008

However, *The Fame* also reflected her diverse (and decidedly often non-pop) taste in music. The playful "Boys Boys Boys" was a deliberate reference to Mötley Crüe's "Girls, Girls, Girls," while "Just Dance" also nodded to her background. "I wanted to do a rock song with big drums but instead of guitars, it's synths," RedOne told *Entertainment Weekly*. "That's what 'Just Dance' is! The opening [synths] are like a guitar chord."

That fresh approach made Gaga's music stand out. In fact, *The Fame* also helped up the BPMs on the pop charts and bring dance-leaning music back into fashion, as high-energy songs by Black Eyed Peas ("I Gotta Feeling," "Boom Boom Pow"), Ke$ha ("TiK ToK"), Flo Rida ("Right Round"), Taio Cruz ("Break Your Heart"), and Far East Movement ("Like a G6") all hit No. 1 in the US, in the wake of Gaga's emergence. That *The Fame* revolutionized modern dance music wasn't necessarily something Gaga saw coming. Not only did she cut her teeth in no-frills dive bars, but she only crossed over to the club scene when she signed a record deal. "I'm making pop records about an underground lifestyle," she said during a 2008 interview.

Thematically, her music also took provocative stances about fame and celebrity—an outsider's view of what it means to be part of society's elite. When talking to *Newsweek* in September 2009, Gaga interrogated the album's themes with provocative, bold statements. "Fame today, the stereotypical idea that we have about fame, is that cameras follow you everywhere and everybody is talking about you and you can't go anywhere. The 'it' girl. [With] *The Fame*, I'm talking about the inner sense of confidence.

"I myself don't like celebrities," she continued. "It's the idea that you can be whoever you want to be. You don't have to be a victim of your environment. You can become the image of yourself you project, [that] you could become in the future."

The Fame's lyrics wrestle with fame's dualities and contradictions in both subtle and direct ways. The title track ticks off various markers of celebrity—Cadillacs, alcohol, "hot blondes in odd positions"—that feel increasingly exaggerated. However, at the end, the song's narrator explicitly declares their ambition to make the goals they've had since adolescence come true. In contrast, "Money Honey" toasts to fame—and celebrates the glitz and glam that comes with it—but realizes it's not what matters; instead, passionate kisses are a much better, worthier goal. And on "Paper Gangsta," which she wrote about the pain of losing her Island Def Jam record deal, she admits the promised land isn't so shiny, and further vows not to get involved with people who don't support her.

The layers of meaning in "Paparazzi" are even more compelling, and hint at more complex songwriting yet to come. "On one level it is about wooing the paparazzi and wanting fame," she said in her official bio that came with *The Fame*. "But it's not to be taken completely seriously. It's about everyone's obsession with that idea." The song was also said to be inspired by her relationship with Lüc Carl, which makes sense given her next point: "[The song is] also about wanting a guy to love you and the struggle of whether you can have success or love—or both."

Gaga's phrasing could be rather unique on *The Fame*; for example, she focused emphasis on odd syllables on "Paper Gangsta." Elsewhere, her descriptive lines put new spins on familiar themes. The lyric "Wish I could shut my Playboy mouth" is a creative way to describe talking dirty; "Poker Face" addressed her bisexuality—she told one audience it was about hiding your lascivious thoughts about a woman because you're with a man; and "LoveGame" boasts the indelible lines "Let's have some fun, this beat is sick / I wanna take a ride on your disco stick." In an interview with *Rolling Stone*, she quipped the naughty phrase is "another of my very thoughtful metaphors for a cock," dreamt up one night while she was out clubbing. "I had quite a sexual crush on somebody, and I said to them, 'I wanna ride on your disco stick.' The next day, I was in the studio, and I wrote the song in about four minutes."

When working with Gaga, Akon recalled a similarly easy and freewheeling vibe, noting every song they wrote together was "done within 30 minutes to an hour. It was all chemistry." He added *The Fame* itself was done in a tidy thirty days—a staggeringly short timeline that included mixing and mastering. "That was another reason I was so excited about working with her, because the ideas and things she sparked were so fresh," Akon continued. "We opened our minds and tried everything. No bars, no barriers, whatever we felt that felt good, whatever we wanted to say, we said it. It was the first time she had no one telling her what she should be doing or how she should be doing it."

Gaga also collaborated on multiple songs with Martin Kierszenbaum, who worked in A&R at Interscope Records and helmed the label Cherrytree. These include the frothy "Eh, Eh (Nothing Else I Can Say)" and the album's disco-punk title track. (The former's "Cherry Cherry Boom Boom," a phrase heard in multiple Gaga songs, is an affectionate nod to Kierszenbaum.) In a 2010 *New York* interview, Kierszenbaum praised Gaga's talent and forward-thinking outlook. "I liked that she was talking about Prince's arrangements, styling, and presentation," he says. "Interest in Prince ebbs and flows, and two years ago, it was very, very maverick. Artists were saying, 'Here's my record and album cover,' not talking about putting screens on the stage."

Of course, Gaga was predisposed to thinking about art in a grandiose way, because as *The Fame* era unfolded, she increasingly used Andy Warhol as a guiding light. She absorbed Warhol's *Before and After I* painting at the

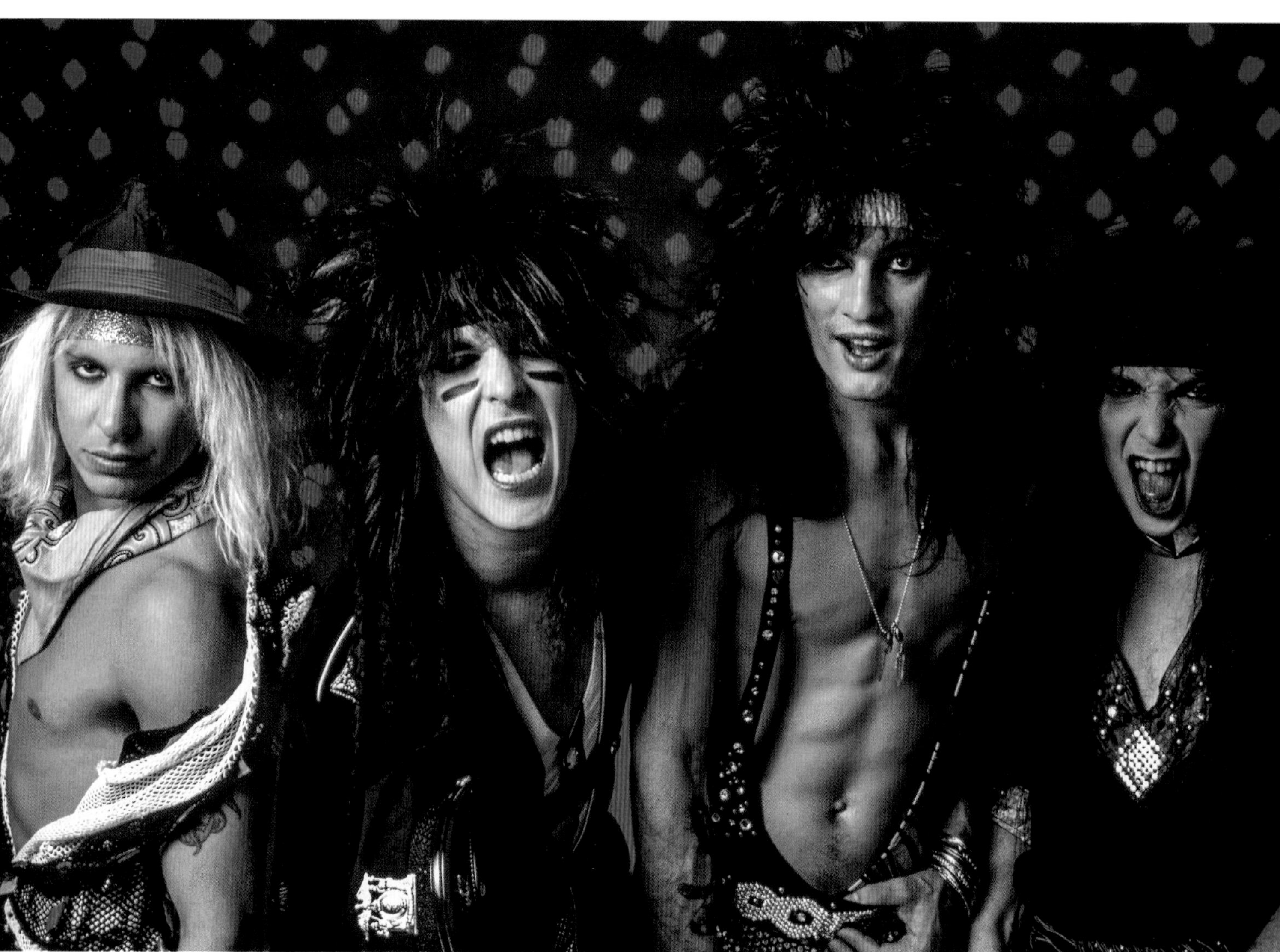

Opposite *Mötley Crüe, 1985. Gaga's "Boys Boys Boys" is a deliberate reference to Mötley Crüe's "Girls, Girls, Girls."*

Above *During* The Fame *era, Andy Warhol served as Gaga's guiding light. According to friend Darian Darling "Andy's books became her bible."*

Metropolitan Museum of Art and devoured books about the noted artist, photographer, writer, and raconteur. "Andy's books became her bible," friend Darian Darling told *New York*. "She would highlight them with a pen." In that same article, Gaga herself invoked Warhol's advice—as well as hairstyle and sunglasses choice—for a confidence boost. "It's as if I've been shouting at everyone, and now I'm whispering and everybody's leaning in to hear me," she said. "I've had to shout for so long because I was only given five minutes, but now I've got fifteen. Andy said you only needed fifteen minutes."

On Valentine's Day 2008, Lady Gaga presented what was called the Lady Gaga Revue, an event she described to one journalist as "a pop show mixed with burlesque and a 70s variety show." During this same interview, she expressed her desire to "revive pop music," and expressed her love for Ace of Base and Swedish pop. "I wanted to do some of that, but bring it back in a way that's new and fresh," she added. "I

Above *Supporting the New Kids on the Block comeback arena tour, at HP Pavilion on October 10, 2008, in San Jose, California*

want people to say, 'That's so Bowie! That's so Berlin! That's so Sonny and Cher!'"

At this point, Gaga was still several months away from releasing "Just Dance," but preparations were well underway for its launch. On March 31, she filmed the song's music video in Los Angeles with director Melina Matsoukas. "For me it was like being on a Martin Scorsese set," Gaga said in an interview with *About.com*. "I've been so low budget for so long, and to have this incredibly amazing video was really very humbling." That doesn't mean the concept was complex, however; Gaga told another interviewer "[t]he whole video is performance art about being drunk at a party."

Indeed, Gaga and a whole troupe of partiers throw the kind of decadent bash that's worth an RSVP: There's karaoke, a DJ, plenty of booze, makeouts, and beautiful people. Gaga naturally is the stylish, fun-loving center of attention thanks to a hip look, including a disco-ball bra and a shiny blue

Above *Lady Gaga at The Roseland Ballroom, New York City, on December 12, 2008*

Left *Sporting a black and gold version of the origami dress, Gaga appears at the New Year's Eve Ball at Webster Hall on December 31, 2008, in New York City*

lightning bolt under her right eye, an homage to her beloved Bowie. If the video for Ke$ha's 2009 hit "TiK ToK" embodied house-destroying debauchery, call Gaga's "Just Dance" the artsy pre-party.

"Just Dance" officially landed in stores on April 8, 2008. The song hit No. 1 in Australia and Canada by the fall, but crossover pop success in the US was elusive; instead, it became merely a dance club hit. Akon for one was frustrated by the lack of open-mindedness at radio. "Everything on the radio sounded exactly the same ... you had a brand new artist coming out with something fresh!" he recalled in a 2018 *Entertainment Weekly* interview. "[When we visited radio stations] I was like, 'I know you guys have a specific playlist that you set up, but can this one record that doesn't sound like anything else be chosen by the audience? Just give us a fair shot!'"

Still, "Just Dance" performed well enough that Gaga nabbed the opening slot on the comeback arena tour by eighties teen-pop heartthrobs New Kids on the Block. She performed a short set before Natasha Bedingfield, who was then riding high on the charts with songs like "Pocketful of Sunshine." Gaga made quite an impression despite being an unknown. "It was apparent to all of us that she was going to be a big star," New Kids on the Block member Joey McIntyre told *Variety* in 2019, adding she was "very warm, collaborative, exciting and inspiring. I don't think any of us were surprised that she has continued to grow as an artist and attracted so many people."

Gaga kept positive about her music—and exuded confidence when talking to journalists. "What I have in common with David Bowie and with Queen and with Prince and with Madonna is the way that I combine theatrics and the visual in all of my performance," she told an Australian website in September 2008. "The fashion and the imagery and what I am trying to say as an artist goes much further beyond the music." However, Gaga stressed she wasn't out to ape these stars or rip off their style. "The intention for me is not to sound just like Bowie or Madonna or Prince. It is to pull references from all of these different people and create something fresh and new and futuristic and pop and different."

Right *Onstage with the Pet Shop Boys at The Brit Awards 2009. (L-R) Neil Tennant, Killers frontman, Brandon Flowers, Lady Gaga, and Chris Lowe*

Although her ambitions were lofty, she still had a long way to go to become a success. *The Fame* was released in late October 2008 in the US and debuted at No. 17 in November, selling a modest 24,000 copies its first week in stores. Still, December 2008 was one of Gaga's most formative months yet. She released a holiday song, "Christmas Tree," and was nominated for her first Grammy Award: "Just Dance" earned a nod for Best Dance Recording. She also met Bruce Springsteen at the Madison Square Garden-held Z100 Jingle Ball. "I climbed over the seats and gave him a big hug, and he told me I was sweet," Gaga told *Rolling Stone*. "Then I had a massive breakdown—I cried on the man's neck!"

Admittedly, her emotions were running high that night anyway: Gaga's first concert ever was the 1998 Z100 Jingle Ball, where she sat in the front row and watched acts such as *NSYNC, Ms. Lauryn Hill and 98° perform. Appearing at the same show a decade later was one impressive full-circle moment. "It's a great story—a New York kid opening for Jingle Ball," Sharon Dastur, program director for radio station WHTZ, told the *New York Daily News*. "When we knew her song was going to be one of the biggest hits on the station, we told her people we wanted her for Jingle Ball, and she burst into tears." Weeks later, she appeared on CNN New Year's Eve performing "Just Dance" while wearing a black version of her asymmetrical origami dress, accented with what looked like gold stalagmites.

Gaga's rocket ride to the top was just beginning. In the UK, "Just Dance" spent three weeks at No. 1 in early 2009. The song was still sitting comfortably at No. 2 when Gaga appeared at the 2009 Brit Awards for a high-profile cameo: Acclaimed synth-pop duo Pet Shop Boys enlisted her to sing Dusty Springfield's iconic contribution to their 1987 hit "What Have I Done to Deserve This?" Wearing a stage outfit that made her resemble an Alice in Wonderland-surreal teacup, she held her own, appearing from the back of the stage with crisp precision and dueting confidently with vocalist Neil Tennant. Gaga didn't carry herself like a new artist: Between her impeccable timing and poised performance, she looked like a seasoned veteran.

After spending the end of 2008 gaining steam, "Just Dance" also topped the US *Billboard* Hot 100 in January 2009. The song took a staggering twenty-two weeks to hit the top spot, and stayed there for three weeks—a nice consolation, since "Just Dance" missed out winning its Grammy, losing the Best Dance Recording category to Daft Punk. The single "saved my life," Gaga told *The Guardian* in 2009. "I was in such a dark space in New York. I was so depressed, always in a bar. I got on a plane to L.A. to do my music and was given one shot to write the song that would change my life and I did." She never looked back—quite literally. "I left behind my boyfriend, my apartment. I still haven't been back. My mother went in and cleared it for me."

Part of that clean break no doubt came from a busy schedule. Gaga spent the first part of 2009 opening for the Pussycat Dolls' Doll Domination tour in the UK and Europe, and then launched her first headline trek, The Fame Ball Tour, in March. Speaking to MTV News, she described this debut

Above *Supporting the Pussycat Dolls on their Doll Domination Tour, in Berlin, Germany, on February 19, 2009*

Right *Lady Gaga performs live during the Fame Ball Tour at House of Blues on March 24, 2009, in Chicago, Illinois*

Right *An explosive performance in Toronto, Canada, at the 20th Annual MuchMusic Video Awards on June 21, 2009*

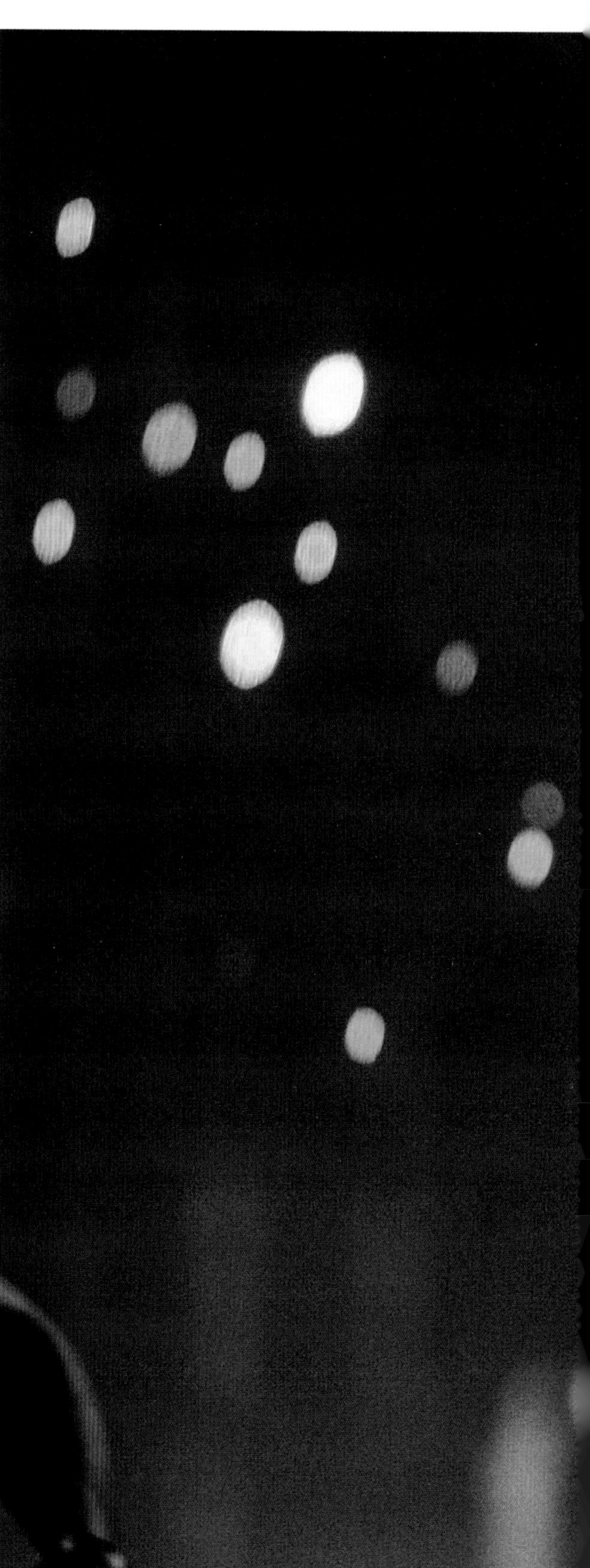

as "more of a traveling party" than a tour, and teased that the show was an immersive, multi-sensory experience. "It's going to be as if you're walking into New York circa 1974," she said. "There's an art installation in the lobby, a DJ spinning your favorite records in the main room, and then the most haunting performance that you've ever seen on the stage."

Gaga was hands-on with planning the night, overseeing every aspect to ensure the party lived up to her exacting expectations. "I'm on the phone every minute of every day, talking to people, being creative, planning this Ball, and my tour manager is constantly saying, 'Come on, we have to go, we've got to go right now,'" she continued. "But to me, the Ball is so important. I want so much to make every depression dollar that everyone spends on my show worth it. And, yeah, I'm paying a lot for it—out of my own pocket. But that's OK. I just don't care about money."

Gaga's insistence on making personal sacrifices for her art would become her calling card in the years to come, as would her workaholic tendencies. "I like doing this all the time. It's my passion," she told *Rolling Stone*. "When I'm not doing a show, I'm writing a song, or I'm on the phone with [creative director Matthew] Dada yapping about a hemline. The truth is, the psychotic woman that I truly am comes out when I'm not working. When I'm not working, I go crazy."

However, the extra effort paid off, as her debut headlining tour, The Fame Ball Tour was an eye-popping multimedia extravaganza. Featuring a loose narrative theme revolving around her alternate persona Candy Warhol, the upbeat show featured interstitial movies, multiple costume changes, sparkly accessories—including a pair of sunglasses encrusted with what looks like disco ball facets and a brassiere that shoots out sparks—and a properly large platform for *The Fame*'s songs.

Her stage props were also top-notch. For example, she commissioned frequent collaborator Tom Talmon Studio to make a literal (light-up) disco stick. "It looks like a giant rock-candy pleasuring tool," she noted lightly to *Rolling Stone*, and later added in liner notes of the deluxe *Book of Gaga*, "We froze acrylic and crushed it with a hammer to make crystals!" "So,

Opposite *Drawing inspiration from British designer Hussein Chalayan, Gaga creates her own bubble dress for a May 2009 performance in Sydney, Australia*

I became the light show and no matter how dark it was in the club, my fans could see me." The stick evolved on future tours to become a disco torch and, much later, a disco scepter and a disco star. Starting on the summer leg of the tour, Gaga also played a sleek, custom black keytar with oversized, crystal-like shapes affixed to the instrument's bottom.

As The Fame Ball Tour marched onward, Gaga proved "Just Dance" was no fluke. In April 2009, she had another US No. 1 hit with "Poker Face," which topped the *Billboard* Hot 100 for one week. Globally, "Poker Face" was also a monster hit, reaching the top of the charts in places such as Australia, Canada and the UK. In the UK, *The Fame* also rose to the top of the Official Albums chart in early April; the album would spend seven non-consecutive weeks at No. 1.

The "Poker Face" video shows off a different, more put-together version of Gaga—the confident pop star, not the reformed club kid. Fittingly, the clip takes place at a fancy mansion with a pool, and the party scenes involve beautiful people playing high-stakes strip poker and making out. Her outfits are also slicker: skintight vinyl with spike heels, an electric-blue leotard with strategic cut-outs, her disco ball-encrusted glasses, a blunt-cut blonde wig.

Gaga also started branching out during TV performances, drawing on her background in theater and classical music. In April, she appeared on *American Idol*, performing "Poker Face" on a clear piano stuffed full of what looked like a string of giant ornamental balls. The performance presaged her later jazz work: Gaga affected a smooth lounge-act voice and dueted on piano with a violinist before switching things up and breaking into the dance version. Even that was different, however: The violinist played along to the brisk BPMs, coming across like a punk-rock orchestral rebel as Gaga threw her body gleefully around the stage.

A May 2009 appearance found her performing "Paparazzi" as a forceful acoustic piece, sitting with her legs crossed at the same clear piano. This version was dramatic and theatrical, like a show-stopping cabaret number, and oozed confidence. For this performance, she wore a bubble dress, constructed by sewing buoyant clear balls to a leotard; the net result was she resembled a bunch of transparent grapes. Gaga dubbed this a "bubble installation" and noted it was based on a dress the British designer Hussein Chalayan had presented in a previous runway show. "I couldn't get the dress, because it's, like, half-a-million dollars in a museum somewhere," she told MTV News, "but I remade it and I built a piano somewhere inspired by it."

The bubble dress reappeared again during Fame Ball Tour live performances, though she made it clear that these out-there fashions had multiple layers of meaning beyond that she wanted to look different. "The methodology behind [my crazy looks] is when they wanted me to be sexy and they wanted me to be pop, I always fucking put some absurd spin on it that made me feel like I was still in control," she said in the 2017 documentary *Five Foot Two*, and told *Rolling Stone* in 2009, "I don't feel that I look like the other perfect little pop singers. I think I look new. I think I'm changing what people think is sexy."

Being freed from conventions was the best thing for her creativity. "Right now the only thing that I am concerned with in my life is being an artist," she told Irish newspaper *The Independent*. "I had to suppress it for so many years in high school because I was made fun of but now I'm completely insulated in my box of insanity and I can do whatever I like."

In June, "LoveGame" became her third Top Five hit in the US For the video, she turned to director Joseph Kahn, who was then known for Britney Spears's "Toxic" and would later leap to even greater heights with his videos for Taylor Swift. Set on a subway and in the subterranean underground, the clip finds Gaga and a variety of characters—leather jacket-clad bikers, police officers, people heading for a night out—dancing and making merry, in a video reminiscent of Michael Jackson's "Bad." Speaking to *Entertainment Weekly*, Gaga said she "wanted to have that big giant dance video moment. I wanted it to be plastic, beautiful, gorgeous, sweaty, tar on the floor, bad-ass boys, but when you got close, the look in everybody's eyes was fucking honest and scary."

Still, her outward confidence wasn't always the same as her inward reality. Speaking to *Rolling Stone* in 2011, she

Opposite *Gaga bleeds to her onstage fake-death in a dramatic performance of "Paparazzi" at the 2009 MTV Video Music Awards*

recalled that this 2009 era was rough for her self-esteem. "Being myself in public was very difficult," she said. "I was being poked and probed, and people would actually touch me and touch my clothes and be like, 'What the fuck is that?,' just so awful. It was like I was being bullied by music lovers, because they couldn't possibly believe that I was genuine. I was too different or too eccentric to be considered sincere."

Indeed, critics could be brutal when writing about Gaga. A review of *The Fame* in *Slant Magazine* observed her "lyrics alternate between cheap drivel and nonsensical drivel, and her vocal performances are uneven at best." A concert review in the *New York Times* observed her music was "an odorless, colorless, almost unnecessary additive to the Lady Gaga spectacle, providing form and little more," while an ultimately positive review in *The Guardian* nevertheless adds, "There's clearly a pretty immense gulf between what Lady Gaga's perception of herself [is] and the reality."

Gaga was also dealing with some tough personal worries while navigating being in the public eye. Her dad's health had started to deteriorate, after years of living with a malfunctioning aortic valve. "His body for a very long time was only pumping a third of the blood that you're supposed to get every time his heart beat," she explained to MTV News. To make matters worse, he was resisting getting open-heart surgery, which would've fixed the issue. "He [was] resigned that he wasn't going to get the surgery and told my mother and I that he was going to let his life take its course," Gaga continued. "And I've been away and on the road and he started to fade when I was gone. My mom called me and I was very depressed."

On the road and unable to come home, she instead channeled her sadness and anxiety into writing a new song called "Speechless." "I wrote this song as a plea to him," she told MTV News. Fittingly, it's a string-laden throwback power ballad that nods to the music with which she grew up: Elton John's lush arrangements and harmonies, seventies rock blazing electric guitars and grooving piano. Gaga then sent the song to her dad, which seemed to have done the trick: Much to her relief, her dad had the needed procedure in October 2009. "After long hours, and lots of tears, they healed his broken heart, and mine. Speechless," she tweeted. "At the hospital. Giving daddy a foot rub while he falls asleep. He's my hero."

Despite these scares, her professional life continued to soar. In September, she won three awards overall at the MTV Video Music Awards, including Best New Artist, and performed "Paparazzi." The four-minute appearance was packed with drama: In front of a stage backdrop that looked like a majestic mansion, she sported half a fur shoulder drape—making it seem like she had a cloud perched on her shoulder—as well as white bikini bottoms and a clingy, belly-baring shirt.

At one point during the song, she sat down at the piano and banged out a mad-scientist classical interlude with her left leg slung over the keyboard. Then, for good measure, she stood up and started spurting fake blood from her chest, before collapsing and then ending the song strung up by one arm over the stage. Camera clicks whirred in the background, signifying figurative paparazzi taking photos of the dead Gaga with the reddish substance smeared all over her face.

The performance was meant to have heavy-handed symbolism, she told MTV News several months later. "I wanted to say something about how the celebrity sort of has this inevitable demise that we love to watch. But are we killing them or are they killing themselves? And do they love the fame and need it but not really want it? And why, when the cameras are there, do they shy away? But if the cameras were there for someone else, would they be jealous?"

Her onstage fake-death was planned in advance, she added—although the channel took a little convincing to make it happen. "I just knew I had to bleed to death for four minutes on TV," she added. "I remember telling MTV, and they were really quiet on the other end of the line. And it was silent, and then they said, 'OK, Gaga, we're gonna make it happen. If that's your vision, were gonna do it.'"

MTV wasn't the only one clamoring for her vision. Thanks to her hit songwriting, she was also beyond thrilled to be asked to write a song for hard rocker-turned-pop crooner

Michael Bolton. "The record label called me and said, 'Michael is doing a new album, and who better to write an '80s love song than Lady Gaga?'" she told *Newsweek*. "I said, 'You're absolutely right.'" She also guested on the resulting song, "Murder My Heart," a soaring mid-tempo duet augmented by strings, piano and pulsating electronic beats. At the behest of Mark Ronson, she co-wrote and sang on "Chillin" by the rapper Wale. "I was happy to do it, but it wasn't really my thing at the time, writing to tracks," she told *Entertainment Weekly* years later. "I was like, 'What is this? How am I going to do this?'"

Much more up her alley was a November appearance on *For Your Entertainment*, the debut album by *American Idol* finalist Adam Lambert. She co-wrote the synth-pop glitterbomb "Fever," which was culled from her pile of existing music that hadn't quite (yet) worked. Although she was already riding high on her success as a solo performer, Gaga was still deeply connected to her humble songwriting

Below *Rapper Eminem looks on in bewilderment as Lady Gaga accepts one of three awards she received at the 2009 MTV Video Music Awards*

roots. "When I do things like this, it's important for me and the artist to remember that I'm not an artist in that room, I'm a songwriter," she told a Dallas radio station, in reference to songwriting for other people. "It's Adam's time and it's his song and I want him to enjoy this moment in his life. You never debut again. You only get one time."

She took that view for her *Saturday Night Live* debut, which featured not just a smoldering performance of "Paparazzi"—Gaga chose a red motif for her outfit, giving her a devilish look—but also acting. The actor Andy Samberg wore a replica of her bubble dress in an absurd skit in which she stretched her chops. And, most notably she appeared in the recurring club/dance spoof sketch "Deep House Dish" alongside guest star Madonna. The women played up their (fake) rivalry, play-fighting and tossing insults at each other. "Guess what, Madonna? I'm totally hotter than you!" Gaga said at one point. Madonna shot back with, "What kind of a name is Lady Gaga? It

Above *Meeting HRH Queen Elizabeth II (L) following the Royal Variety Performance in Blackpool, UK, on December 7, 2009*

Opposite, top *Lady Gaga makes her* Saturday Night Live *debut in a spoof sketch with guest star Madonna (R)* **Opposite, bottom** *Gaga's outfits become ever more complex. At the Royal Variety Performance in December 2009, she plays on a piano suspended in the air, while wearing a red latex dress with a twenty-foot train.*

sounds like baby food, to which Gaga responded, "The kind that's No. 1 on the *Billboard* chart!"

Weeks later, "Paparazzi" would become her fourth Top Ten US single, reaching No. 6 on the *Billboard* Hot 100. The song featured her most elaborate music video yet. Directed by Jonas Åkerlund and co-starring actor Alexander Skarsgård as Gaga's boyfriend, it underscored the song's lyrical themes. "It has a real, genuine, powerful message about fame-whoring and death and the demise of the celebrity, and what that does to young people," she told *The Canadian Press*. "The video explores ideas about sort of hyperbolic situations that people will go to in order to be famous—most specifically, pornography and murder."

Indeed, the clip starts with Skarsgård pushing Gaga over a balcony in a fit of anger. She survives and comes back to life using a wheelchair and then space-age crutches. Throughout the video, Gaga sports a variety of outrageous outfits as she plots out her revenge and warns of fame's hubris. These fashions include a gold-plated bustier with matching briefs, and neck and wrist cuffs—in truth, she looks like the *Star Wars* robot C-3PO with body armor missing—as well as a black vinyl dress, and an all-white bodysuit with gray-and-black plumed accents. The video culminates with her wearing a skin-tight yellow bodysuit with cartoonish mouse heads (think a cross between deadmau5 and Mickey Mouse) and sunglasses with multiple circular lenses. Calmly, and with absolutely no remorse, she poisons Skarsgård—finally achieving the infamy she craves.

As the year wound down, Gaga's outfits became ever more complex. In December, she played at the Royal Variety Performance in Blackpool on a piano suspended in the air, while wearing a red latex dress with puffy sleeves, an Elizabethan neck ruffle and a twenty-foot train. Photos showed her meeting Queen Elizabeth II while looking like a club-kid raccoon, her eyes ringed with glittering red makeup. On New Year's Eve, Gaga rang in 2010 at the James L. Knight Center in Miami—and, for good measure, ended 2009 by having the best-selling digital song of the year, as "Poker Face" sold 9.8 million copies worldwide. That wasn't the only bit of good news that emerged: Gaga was also nominated for multiple Grammys, including Song of the Year and Record of the Year for "Poker Face," and the prestigious Album of the Year for *The Fame*.

In her official bio released with *The Fame*, Gaga was reflective but defiant about her burgeoning success. "I did this the way you are supposed to. I played every club in New York City and I bombed in every club and then killed it in every club and I found myself as an artist. I learned how to survive as an artist, get real, and how to fail and then figure out who I was as singer and performer. And I worked hard." The bio ended on a kicker, noting that Gaga winked and said: "And, now, I'm just trying to change the world one sequin at a time."

Still, even at this early stage, she demonstrated creative restlessness—and a strong desire to avoid Warhol's fifteen-minute fame trap. "I feel like I have so much to do," she told *Rolling Stone* in 2009. "The whole world sees the number-one records and the rise in sales and recognition, but my true legacy will be the test of time, and whether I can sustain a space in pop culture and really make stuff that will have a genuine impact."

"I played every club in New York City and I bombed in every club and then killed it in every club and I found myself as an artist."

LADY GAGA

GAGA HAUS OF FASHION

Lady Gaga's early fashions and cutting-edge stage props emerged from her creative brain trust, Haus of Gaga. The collective, which was modeled after Andy Warhol's bohemian oasis The Factory, was akin to an artistic Wrecking Crew; initial members included the French producer Space Cowboy; choreographer Laurieann Gibson; stylist Bea Åkerlund; fashion director Nicola Formichetti; and creative director Matthew Williams nicknamed "Matty Dada."

Gaga viewed this collective as a way to make her ambitious visual aesthetic a reality. "I called all my coolest art friends and we sat in a room and I said that I wanted to make my face light up," she told MTV. "Or that I wanted to make my cane light up. Or that I wanted to make a pair of dope sunglasses. Or that I want to make video glasses, or whatever it was that I wanted to do. It's a whole amazing creative process that's completely separate from the [record] label."

The Haus smartly looked outside themselves for collaborators. Early on, Gaga's team reached out to Glenn Hetrick, a make-up artist and costume designer who would later win a Primetime Emmy Award for his work on *Star Trek: Discovery*, and hired him to build "techno futuristic armor," with "different versions of it for different performances," he recalled to *SciFi Vision*. At the time he met with a member of Gaga's team, she was still unknown; in fact, Hetrick had no idea who she was. "I'd never heard of her," he recalled. "And [the Gaga team member] sort of went, very assuredly, 'It's okay, no one has yet, but she's about to get huge.'"

Sure enough, different versions of Hetrick's molded armor became a familiar presence during Gaga's *The Fame*-era performances as her profile soared. There were different varieties: gold, silver, metal, clear, and a version with a fancy blue pattern that might be imprinted on a delicate set of dishware. This form-fitting Gaga armor was futuristic, fashionable and cinematic—the embodiment of her aesthetic.

At this stage, her wicked sense of humor and homegrown fashion sense still loomed large. On the homage front, she told *The Guardian* that Marc Bolan's "full-body scuba suit covered in mirrors" inspired the angular and reflective disco ball dress she wore onstage. During an appearance on *The Ellen DeGeneres Show* and on the cover of *V magazine*, she sported a headpiece that looked like overlapping electron orbits; on *Saturday Night Live*, she wore a blown-out version of the hat around her body that resembled intersecting hula-hoops.

In 2009, she unveiled another infamous fashion choice, appearing on a German television show wearing a fluffy jacket embroidered with a full fleet of Kermit the Frog puppets and a matching beret comprised of a sickly-looking Kermit head. "I thought it was comical because I don't wear fur," she told *Newsweek*. "But there was something morbid and hilarious and wearing a jacket made of lots of Kermits. Dead, dead Kermits."

Yet after the elaborate video for "Paparazzi," the upscale fashion world took notice of her creativity and potential. "Gaga had some archival pieces from Thierry Mugler, but after 'Paparazzi,' everything changed," an ex-Haus of Gaga member told *New York*. "It happened in the blink of an eye. Suddenly, every fashion designer in the world was e-mailing her images."

Above and opposite *Futuristic, fashionable, and cinematic. Gaga's early outfits were the brainchild of costume designer Glenn Hetrick*

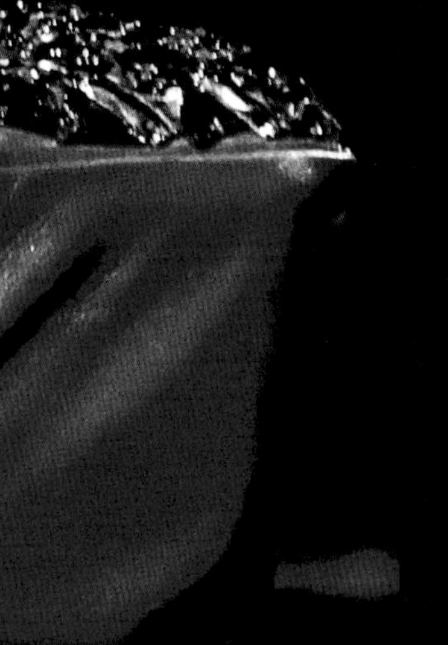

THE FAME MONSTER

Previous spread *Lady Gaga performs at Lollapalooza on August 6, 2010, in Grant Park, Chicago, Illinois*

Opposite *Making an entrance at The 2010 Brit Awards*

"It's yin and yang. It's 'This is how I feel. I feel divided. I feel a dichotomy within myself. I am ready for the future, but I mourn the past.'"
LADY GAGA

Gaga's momentum kept snowballing as the calendar flipped to 2010. Not only did *The Fame* reach its peak of No. 2 on the *Billboard* 200 albums chart in mid-January, but she also had another release in the Top Ten that same week: a standalone EP called *The Fame Monster* featuring eight brand-new tracks.

She returned to the Brit Awards in 2010 as a solo artist, sporting a lace slip over the top half of her face and a Marie Antoinette-like wig that resembled a perfect cotton candy puff. She first dedicated a brittle piano version of "Telephone" to the memory of one of her idols, the fashion designer Alexander McQueen, and then pumped up the electro beats for an avant-garde take on "Dance In The Dark." On January 31, she won her first two Grammy Awards: Best Dance/Electronica Album for *The Fame*, and Best Dance Recording for "Poker Face."

Gaga also opened the awards show with a barn-burning performance. Wearing a sea-green Armani leotard with puffed shoulders and fins at her hip—making her look like a whimsical fish—she danced first to "Poker Face" and then dueted with Elton John on her "Speechless" and his "Your Song." For the latter part of her Grammy Awards performance, she played a Baldwin piano customized by Terence Koh, that featured forearms with claw-like hands protruding from the top. Although the instrument resembled something out of a horror movie—say, newly minted zombies thrusting their arms up from the ground—the arms actually represented her fans. The decor was deeply meaningful, as Gaga's blockbuster 2009 had helped her start to amass an army of loyal fans dubbed "Little Monsters."

Every major pop star has a fanbase with a cute nickname: Taylor Swift has Swifties, BTS has ARMY, Ariana Grande has Arianators, Katy Perry has KatyCats, Beyoncé has the Beyhive. However, in the wake of *The Fame*, the Little Monsters fanbase started to grow and take on a life of its own. Gaga's proclamations of misfitdom and being an outsider resonated

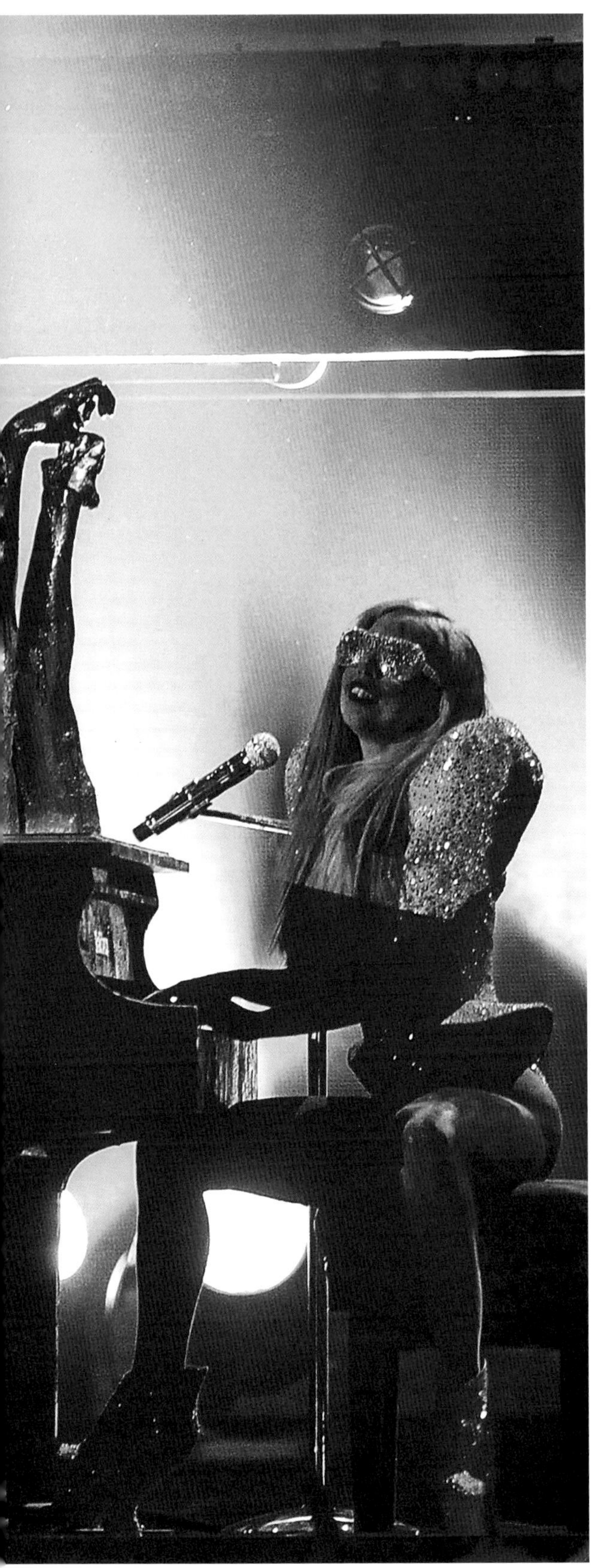

Left *Dueting with Elton John (L) on a piano customized by Terence Koh, at the 52nd Annual Grammy Awards. The zombie-esque arms represent Gaga's fans, Little Monsters.*

deeply: Her fans created art, wore elaborate costumes to concerts and mimicked their idol's stage moves, such as the claw-like paw she'd throw up like a sign of solidarity. They'd also have visceral reactions to her music and lyrics, picking up on the deeper themes and finding solace (and solidarity) in Gaga's honesty.

In the luxe *Book of Gaga*, which was packaged with a super deluxe version of *The Fame Monster*, the star outlined something she called the "Manifesto of Little Monsters." The brief missive positioned her fans as the ones with power:

"There's something heroic about the way my fans operate their cameras. So precisely and intricately, so proudly, and so methodically. Like Kings writing the history of their people. It's their prolific nature that both creates and procures what will later be perceived as the 'kingdom.' So, the real truth about Lady Gaga fans lies in this sentiment: They are the kings. They are the queens. They write the history of the kingdom, while I am something of a devoted Jester."

This statement flips the script on the usual royal relationship, where the jester is a comedian meant to keep the king and queen happy. Instead, Gaga asserted she wasn't some pop star on a pedestal: She empowered her fans, tipping the balance so *they* were the royals she was keeping entertained. That was no accident, as it was clear she viewed the musician-fan dynamic as a mutually beneficial relationship. "I love what they stand for," she told *Rolling Stone*. "I love who they are. They inspire me to be more confident every day. When I wake up in the morning, I feel just like any other insecure 24-year-old girl. But I say, 'Bitch, you're Lady Gaga, you better fucking get up and walk the walk today,' because they need that from me. And they inspire me to keep going."

Gaga kept the Little Monsters satisfied with the late 2009 release of *The Fame Monster*, which ended up being somewhere between an addition and a sequel to *The Fame*. (To confuse matters, fans could also buy a double album deluxe edition with *The Fame* and bonus tracks on the B-side.) As The Fame Monster's name implies, her inspiration was quite different this time around: darker, more ominous, slightly scary. "I have an obsession with death and sex," she said in July

2009, adding she had also been "obsessing over" horror films and also watching science fiction movies from the 1950s, all due to the impending release of *The Fame Monster*.

"I've just been sort of bulimically eating and regurgitating monster movies and all things scary. I've just been noticing a resurgence of this idea of monster, of fantasy, but in a very real way." Gaga also pointed out one of the more overlooked facets of horror movies: "If you notice in those films, there's always a juxtaposition of sex with death. That's what makes it so scary. Body and mind are primed for orgasm and instead somebody gets killed. That's the sort of sick, twisted psychological circumstance."

Although *The Fame* and *The Fame Monster* share collaborators, including RedOne and Space Cowboy, the music is already edging into another galaxy. There's the slow-burning power ballad "Speechless," of course, as well as nods to high-stepping Broadway razzmatazz ("Teeth"), sultry ballroom dancing ("Alejandro"), and eighties dance-pop ("Dance In The Dark"). Gaga's newer songs also exude greater lyrical sophistication and depth. Her wordplay is more clever especially on "Dance In The Dark" (the line "Her kiss is a vampire grin," as well as lyrics that rhyme "tramp" with "vamp"), although these turns of phrase don't obscure the song's heartbreak: The concept of dancing in the dark seems to be cover for insecurities and an imperfect relationship. "Telephone," a song Gaga originally wrote for Britney Spears's *Circus* album, captures the agony and ecstasy

Above *Little Monsters in Sydney, Australia*

"I love who they are. They inspire me to be more confident every day. When I wake up in the morning, I feel just like any other insecure 24-year-old girl. But I say, 'Bitch, you're Lady Gaga, you better fucking get up and walk the walk today,' because they need that from me." LADY GAGA

of miscommunication (or no communication), while the de facto title track, "Monster," likens an all-consuming romantic relationship to getting entangled with a zombie: "He ate my heart and then he ate my brain."

"I wrote about everything I didn't write on *The Fame*," she said in a statement tied to the album's release. "While traveling the world for two years, I've encountered several monsters, each represented by a different song on the new record: my 'Fear of Sex Monster,' my 'Fear of Alcohol Monster,' my 'Fear of Love Monster,' my 'Fear of Death Monster,' my 'Fear of Loneliness Monster.'"

Fittingly, she told MTV that she insisted to her record label that the aesthetic and cover of *The Fame Monster* should be darker, less polished. Mission accomplished: The EP's cover is a black-and-white photo of Gaga hugging a black vinyl jacket around herself while wearing a blunt-cut, triangular blonde wig. Unlike the star-kissed visage seen on *The Fame*, her look here is solemn and mysterious.

"It's yin and yang. It's 'This is how I feel. I feel divided. I feel a dichotomy within myself. I am ready for the future, but I mourn the past,'" she explained. "And it's a very real rite of passage—you have to let go of things. You have to mourn them like a death so that you can move on, and that's sort of what the album is about."

The videos for this album also upped Gaga's game, starting with the clip for lead single "Bad Romance." She worked with Francis Lawrence, who directed 2007's *I Am Legend*, because of his open-minded style. "I knew he could execute the video in a way that I could give him all my weirdest, most psychotic ideas," Gaga told MTV News. "But it would come across to and be relevant to the public." More important, she felt Lawrence viewed her as an equal-opportunity collaborator. "I wanted somebody with a tremendous understanding of how to make a pop video, because my biggest challenge working with directors is that I am the director and I write the treatments and I get the fashion and I decide what it's about and it's very hard to find directors that will relinquish any sort of input from the artist."

"Bad Romance" is a compact look at Gaga's themes from this era: the perils of fame, female empowerment, revenge and atonement, embracing the spotlight on your own terms. Setting-wise, it's a cross between a sci-fi film set in the distant future and a James Bond-caliber espionage film, along with a dash of fashion world drama. "There's this one shot in the video where I get kidnapped by supermodels," Gaga told MTV News. "I'm washing away my sins and they shove vodka down my throat to drug me up before they sell me off to the Russian mafia."

The video starts with Gaga and a cadre of dancers—all of whom sport skintight white-latex outfits with monster-esque head adornments—emerging from pods at the "Bath Haus of Gaga" and doing synchronized moves. "I was obsessed with Chubby Checker and old dances, like the twist," choreographer Laurieann Gibson told *Us Weekly* in 2010. "So when I heard 'Bad Romance,' we just twisted it out and then we added the hand. It's based on the twist." These moments represent just one of Gaga's personas, of course. At one point, she's alien-like, with cartoonish oversized eyes and a pink-streaked curly blonde wig; at another point, she's a burned-out fashion icon with trapezoidal razor-blade sunglasses and an eighties throwback gold dress. In the end, Gaga ends up in a skimpy lingerie set, setting fire to the man who's attempted to purchase her—a nod that nobody owns her.

Right *Lady Gaga (L) and Beyoncé (R) in the Tarantino-esque music video for "Telephone." Tarantino loaned Gaga the Pussy Wagon*

Above *With Madonna (R) at the Marc Jacobs 2010 Spring Fashion Show*

Opposite *Performing onstage during the Monster Ball Tour at Nokia Theatre L.A. Live in Los Angeles, California, on December 22, 2009*

The nine-minute cinematic epic "Telephone" was even more elaborate. Directed by Jonas Åkerlund, who also helmed the clip for "Paparazzi," the video finds Gaga and Beyoncé updating the story of Bonnie and Clyde, as seen through the noir lens of Quentin Tarantino. (Literally: Beyoncé's character is named "Honey Bee"—a *Pulp Fiction* reference—and Tarantino was so into the video's plot and theme he lent the crew the Pussy Wagon from the film *Kill Bill: Volume 1*.) The video's colors are blown-out and oversaturated, and there's a spoof-like quality to the dialogue and scenes.

"There was this really amazing quality in 'Paparazzi,' where it kind of had this pure pop music quality but at the same time it was a commentary on fame culture," Gaga told E! News, while praising Åkerlund's "high-art quality" filming approach. "I wanted to do the same thing with this video—take a decidedly pop song, which on the surface has a quite shallow meaning, and turn it into something deeper."

"Telephone" indeed has a well-scripted plot that serves as a sequel to "Paparazzi," a video that ended with Gaga under arrest for killing her boyfriend. Here, Gaga first portrays a punk-rock prisoner decked out in leather and chains, as if she's a wayward extra from *Grease*. (In one scene, she actually wears a headset comprised of lit cigarettes.) She's bailed out of jail by Beyoncé, and the two hit the road and head to a diner, where they proceed to poison everyone's food and then flee the town together.

However, "Telephone" also doubles as pointed social critique—the women wear clothes adorned with the American flag while gleefully doing dances to celebrate the deaths of diner patrons—and a nod to the ways technology makes life more difficult. In fact, Gaga later shared with E! News that the video addresses "the idea that America is full of young people that are inundated with information and technology and turn it into something that was more of a commentary on the kind of country that we are."

From a thematic and cinematography standpoint, *The Fame Monster*'s next major video, "Alejandro" is the complete opposite of "Telephone." Directed by photographer Steven Klein, who is known for his stylized high-fashion photos, the clip has a "homoerotic military theme," Gaga told Larry King during an appearance on CNN. "It is a celebration of my love and appreciation for the gay community, my admiration of their bravery, their love for one another and their courage in their relationships." Klein uses dim lighting and darker hues, as well as stylized choreography that references the intersection of faith, religion and sexuality.

Madonna, with whom Klein had collaborated on art projects, is also an obvious touchstone; the video nods to iconic moments found in the Material Girl's "Vogue" and "Express Yourself" videos.

The Catholic League for one picked up on the parallels between Madonna and Gaga in the stark video. President Bill Donohue issued a scathing statement calling Gaga a "Madonna copy-cat, squirming around half-naked with half-naked guys" and "abusing Catholic symbols ... while bleating out 'Alejandro' enough times to induce vomit." The statement further criticized the pop star for invoking the cross, swallowing a rosary and "manag[ing] to get raped by her S&M boyfriends," and added, "She has now become the new poster girl for American decadence and Catholic bashing, sans the looks and talent of her role model."

Gaga was far too busy working to worry about offending anyone, however. She plotted a major big-venue tour with Kanye West, dubbed Fame Kills: Starring Kanye West and Lady Gaga, that was due to start in fall 2009. However, this trek ended up not happening after West decided to take a break instead—and, in November 2009, she launched The Monster Ball Tour to support *The Fame Monster*.

In many ways, it was a bigger, more expansive version of The Fame Ball Tour. For example, she had several oversized keytars shaped like a pyramid that were described by artistic

Opposite *The Monster Ball Tour comes to Staples Center in Los Angeles, California, on August 11, 2010* **Above** *At the Trent FM Arena on May 27, 2010, in Nottingham, UK*

Previous spread *Playing a keyboard built into the hood of a crashed car, during the Monster Ball Tour at the O2 Arena in London, UK, on February 26, 2010* **Opposite** *Gaga plays "EMMA"—an instrument incorporating a bass guitar, a synthesizer and a drum machine, custom-made by Glenn Hetrick*

collaborator Glenn Hetrick as "almost M.C. Escheresque" in design. "And we did a clear version with internal blacklighting and we did a purple version of that." Her disco stick was now a blazing disco torch with strobe light capabilities.

And, perhaps most impressive, she had a custom instrument named "EMMA" she played during "The Fame" that incorporated a bass guitar, a synthesizer and a drum machine. Hetrick likened it to a stand-up bass with intricate, steampunk-like features. "I made it sort of very antique Victorian," he said. "It's all rosewood with lots of brass inlays and hand-etched items all over it as decoration. The instruments were a completely new experiment for us." Gaga wasn't afraid of experimentation, of course, but her willingness to create entirely new ways to play music reflects her expanded confidence and worldview—and her love of working with equally forward-thinking collaborators.

Conceptually, The Monster Ball Tour was a "pop-electro opera" with a broad scope and a cohesive plot, she told *Rolling Stone*. "The theatrics and story elements are in the style of an opera. Imagine if you could take the sets of an opera, which are very grand and very beautiful, and put them through a pop-electro lens." That vibe is evident on the show's darkwave-synthpop opener, "Dance In The Dark," which felt very eighties: Gaga sang the song in silhouette, within a cityscape backdrop full of neon signs, and a few songs later played "Just Dance" on a keyboard built into the hood of a crashed car, while wearing a Day-Glo yellow wig and purple leotard.

However, Gaga built the show around a theme of "evolution," which she said hewed to what *The Fame Monster* itself was about. "I don't write about fame or money at all on this new record. So we talked about monsters and how, I believe, that innately we're all born with the monsters already inside of us—I guess in Christianity they call it original sin—the prospect that we will, at some point, sin in our lives, and we will, at some point, have to face our own demons, and they're already inside of us." As the night progressed, Gaga nodded to gory zombie movies ("Monster," performed while surrounded by undead-like dancers), sported an ethereal white dress studded with icicle-like spikes and a matching diaphanous headdress ("So Happy I Could Die") and stripped down to a black-leather bikini for a solo piano version of "Speechless" that featured flames burning atop the instrument.

The Monster Ball Tour was "one of the most critical moments of my life" to date, she later told *Rolling Stone*. "I've realized that my purpose on the Earth is so much greater than writing hit songs. There's something about my relationship with my fans that's so pure and genuine. During the show, I say, 'I don't lip-sync, and I never will, because it is in my authenticity that you can know the sincerity of my love for you. I love you so much that I sweat blood and tears in the mirror every day, dancing, writing music, to become better for you to be a leader, to be strong and brave, not to follow.'"

As the tour progressed, Gaga also collected more awards and accolades. "Bad Romance" topped the charts in Canada and the UK, and peaked at No. 2 in the US, Australia and New Zealand, while "Telephone" also topped the UK singles charts, giving Gaga her impressive fourth No. 1 to date there. Three years after her low-key daytime set, she headlined Lollapalooza. "Bad Romance" became what was then the most-viewed YouTube video ever—it racked up an impressive-for-2010, 179 million views—and in October Gaga became the first artist to crack one billion overall views on the platform.

On September 12, 2010, she wore her infamous meat dress to the MTV Video Music Awards, where she was nominated a record-setting thirteen times and won eight awards, including Video of the Year for "Bad Romance." Over the course of 2010, a remix album (called, simply, *The Remix*) saw a release around the world. And in early 2011, *The Fame Monster* won the Grammy Award for Best Pop Vocal Album, while "Bad Romance" won two awards: Best Female Pop Vocal Performance and Best Short Form Music Video.

Still, the monster side of the business reared its ugly head as Gaga's star ascended. On March 10, 2010, Rob Fusari filed a $30.5 million lawsuit against her in Manhattan state court. "All business is personal," the suit said, and outlined how he was allegedly instrumental in shaping Gaga's look, style, music, approach, and even name. Although Fusari had production

Left *Gaga plays one of several oversized pyramid shaped keytars made especially for The Monster Ball Tour, at a show in Birmingham, UK*

and songwriting credits on *The Fame*, the lawsuit claimed he was owed (among other things) further song royalties and merchandising revenue. Gaga countersued him, although both parties reached a settlement in September 2010. (While terms were kept confidential, tabloids reported years later that Gaga allegedly paid him millions, plus future royalties.) That same month, Wendy Starland filed a lawsuit against Fusari and his business, alleging breach of contract, breach of fiduciary duty and unjust enrichment because Fusari hadn't given her a promised share of revenues from Gaga's success.

Lawsuits often go hand-in-hand with fame, as people disagree with who should benefit from material success. However, Gaga didn't dwell on these legal distractions. Instead, she continued looking ahead and started laying the groundwork for her next album, *Born This Way*. In fact, she was already deep into working on new music in early 2010, while she was still on tour promoting *The Fame* and *The Fame Monster*. "I've already written the core of [*Born This Way*] so I'm just continuing to travel around the world and make something really great," she told Australian radio station 2DayFM in March of that year. "It's certainly my best work to date."

Speaking to *The Times* a few months later, she referenced recently having had a "miracle-like experience, where I feel much more connected to God," and noted the forthcoming *Born This Way* was "more spiritual." Gaga demurred on specifics, but did drop some hints of the album's themes. "I will say that religion is very confusing for everyone, and particularly me, because there's really no religion that doesn't hate or condemn a certain kind of people, and I totally believe in all love and forgiveness, and excluding no one."

And while wearing her infamous meat dress at the MTV Video Music Awards, she gave fans an official tease of *Born This Way* while accepting her Video of the Year award for "Bad Romance." She announced the album's title and sang a snippet of the title track: "I'm beautiful in my way, 'cause God makes no mistakes / I'm on the right track, baby, I was born this way." Indefatigable optimism in the face of insurmountable odds—it's the Lady Gaga way.

THE MEAT OUTFIT

No discussion of Lady Gaga's fashion is complete without a deep dive into the meat dress she wore at the 2010 MTV Video Music Awards. An outfit so infamous that it has its own lengthy Wikipedia entry, it caused controversy, but also cemented her legacy as one of the most adventurous fashionistas of all time. After all, nobody else but Gaga would think to go to an awards show dressed head-to-toe in raw meat—chunky platform boots, an asymmetrical dress, a jaunty beret, and a purse.

Even without the outfit, Gaga would've made waves at this particular MTV Video Music Awards. She previewed a teaser of the title track of her next album, *Born This Way*, during the show, and for much of the night, she looked radiant wearing works by Alexander McQueen and Giorgio Armani. Argentine designer Franc Fernandez and Gaga's stylist Nicola Formichetti oversaw the meat dress, her third and final outfit of the night.

There was some precedent for her all-meat outfit, as she sported a "meat bikini" on the cover of the magazine *Vogue Hommes Japan*. However, this particular thirty-five-pound carnivorous concept came together in a week and was made from matambre, a thinly sliced cut of beef Fernandez bought from his family's favored butcher shop in Granada Hills, California. The meat was a bargain, with a price of around $3.99 per pound. "There's been a big debate of whether it smelled or rotted under the lights," Fernandez told MTV News. "Gaga herself said it smelled good, because it smelled like meat. I chose the right cuts to make sure the dress kept well."

Indeed, matambre isn't bloody or smelly, which was appealing to Fernandez, although styling the dress did pose some challenges. "Working with meat as a material requires you to do it last minute," he told *StyleList*; in fact, the dress had to be pieced and sewn together while Gaga was wearing it. "I knew the dress would be one of other amazing pieces Gaga wore that night," he told *Huffington Post*. "It's very well made and looked great on her, on and off camera. We didn't get a chance to have a fitting. The only time she had it on was for the VMAs. Only when I saw it in the monitor did I know it would be big."

Indeed, Gaga certainly turned heads when she accepted the award for Video of the Year from Cher while wearing the outfit. "I never thought I'd be asking Cher to hold my meat purse," Gaga said in her speech.

Above and opposite
At the 2010 MTV Video Music Awards wearing the now legendary meat dress

Cher ultimately approved of the bold move, tweeting, "The way it was cut & fitted to her body was AMAZING! Meat purse was genius! As art piece it was astonishing! No moral judgement!"

As might be expected, Gaga's dress wasn't meant as a pro-animal rights gesture; instead, it signified something deeper, the pop star told Ellen DeGeneres during an interview after the awards. It had to do with the people who accompanied her to the awards that night: former US military members who were discharged due to the "Don't Ask, Don't Tell" policy: "It is a devastation to me that I know my fans who are gay ... feel like they have governmental oppression on them. That's actually why I wore the meat tonight."

Gaga clarified to DeGeneres that she meant "no disrespect to anyone that's vegan or vegetarian" with the outfit. "As you know, I'm the most judgment-free human being on the Earth. It has many interpretations, but for me this evening it's [saying], 'If we don't stand up for what we believe in, if we don't fight for our rights, pretty soon we're going to have as much rights as the meat on our bones.'" (DeGeneres, who is vegan, jokingly gave Gaga some clothes made of kale so she'd be prepared "the next time you want to pose in a bikini somewhere," she quipped.)

Unsurprisingly, PETA (People for the Ethical Treatment of Animals), wasn't buying Gaga's explanation, and swiftly and sternly condemned her outfit. "Wearing a dress made out of cuts of dead cows is offensive enough to bring comment," the organization said in a statement. "But someone should whisper in her ear that there are more people who are upset by butchery than who are impressed by it—and that means a lot of young people will not be buying her records if she keeps this stuff up."

The dress was preserved as jerky and later displayed at the Rock and Roll Hall of Fame in Cleveland, Ohio, as part of the "Women Who Rock: Vision, Passion, Power" exhibit. Making that happen was also laborious: According to the *Los Angeles Times*, the museum reportedly paid taxidermist Sergio Vigilato $6,000 to carefully prepare the dress to ensure it could be displayed.

"The first thing I asked was, 'Where is the dress? This thing could have maggots by now,'" Vigilato told the newspaper, recalling when he was asked to handle the dress. "I understood them to say it was in a room with air conditioning. I said make sure it's in a freezer." Luckily, it was frozen then—although, unfortunately, it had started decomposing at some point along the way and had started to smell. Vigilato spent months cleaning and preserving the meat so it would be museum-ready.

Gaga herself wore a meat-free replica of the dress on the Born This Way Ball tour for the songs "Americano" and "Poker Face." And while the Rock Hall exhibit was an achievement, she received an even bigger honor: "Weird Al" Yankovic wrote a parody song about her, "Perform This Way," and wore a version of the meat dress in the tune's video.

BORN THIS WAY

Previous spread *Lady Gaga shows support for Italy's gay community during the 2011 Europride in Rome*

Opposite *Performing at gay club Nevermind in Sydney, Australia, on July 11, 2011*

"I just like to keep people around me that remind me of what I think is going to be, ultimately, part of my greater legacy."
LADY GAGA

When *Rolling Stone* interviewed Lady Gaga in 2010, she was deep into superhuman-superstar mode. "I don't want people to see I'm a human being," she said. "I don't even drink water onstage in front of anybody, because I want them to focus on the fantasy of the music and be transported from where they are to somewhere else. People can't do that if you're just on Earth. We need to go to heaven."

A year later, when *Rolling Stone* caught up with Gaga again, at the tail-end of her Monster Ball Tour, her tone was different. She was already cognizant of her growing place in music history. Backstage in Nashville, the writer Brian Hiatt talked to her as she sat underneath photos of rock greats: Led Zeppelin guitarist Jimmy Page, Blondie lead singer Debbie Harry, punk bands the Sex Pistols and the Ramones, and two rock 'n' roll icons: John Lennon and Elvis Presley.

"I just like to keep people around me that remind me of what I think is going to be, ultimately, part of my greater legacy, as opposed to committing myself to a trend or to an idea of what the public perceives my music or my artistry or personality to be," she said by way of explanation. "It reminds me to be myself."

Indeed, while it's fair to say Gaga has always been aggressively herself, The Monster Ball Tour brought about a marked shift toward a more personal creative outlook. She started writing deeply felt songs ("Speechless") and performed an unreleased song called "Glitter And Grease" that made direct reference to her on-again, off-again boyfriend Lüc Carl. In interviews, she also started opening up more, pairing her usual sassy, savvy soundbites with earnest political and social activism.

Part of this shift of course had to do with her loyal Little Monsters. Speaking to *SHOWstudio.com*, she noted her *Born This Way*-era songwriting boasted "this new instinctual energy that I've developed getting to know my fans. They

protect me, so now it's now my destiny to protect them ... Particularly with my next album, I'm much more self-aware of my spiritual and leadership connection to my little monsters and the world in the way that any artist is a leader in that way."

Less than a year after her dad's health scare with his heart, Gaga experienced an immense loss in her personal life. On September 24, 2010, her paternal grandfather, Joseph—one-half of the couple that had bought the piano that transformed her life—died at the age of eighty-eight. "I don't always talk about my personal life but my grandpa's sick," she had told the crowd the previous May at a show in Nottingham, in the UK, before dedicating "Speechless" to him. "And I'm really close with my grandpa and he's really sick and he's in the States and my dad's with him. So I was, like, crying all day, really sad. So I thought I might just be honest and tell you that's what's going on."

Circa *Born This Way*, Gaga also started looking back and analyzing the origins of her past destructive behaviors, in hopes of finding understanding and healing. One of her realizations was that being bullied growing up had a deeper impact than she had appreciated. "It was something so painful," she says. "This huge wound that had been inside

"I just have so much respect for my friends who live bisexual lives and who live transgender lives and who every single day have to fight for their identity and have to deal with all the things that come along with sexual orientation."
LADY GAGA

Opposite *Lady Gaga speaks to the crowd during the #4the14K Rally protesting the military's "Don't Ask, Don't Tell" policy, in Portland, Maine, on September 20, 2010*

of me for so long that I had buried in drugs and alcohol and older men and over and over in a cycle of just unhappiness with myself and looking outward to fix it, to numb it. My fans forced me to respond to it."

All of these things poured into her songwriting for *Born This Way*, which was more declarative and defiant than the music she had released to date. "*Born This Way* is my answer to many questions over the years: Who are you? What are you about?," she told *The Metro* newspaper. "The most paramount theme on the record is me struggling to understand how I can exist as myself as someone who lives halfway between fantasy and reality all the time."

If this seems like an extension of *The Fame Monster*, that's partly true—but instead of scary movies or monster films, *Born This Way* interrogated real life, which can be equally frightening. Speaking to *Huffington Post*, Gaga reiterated her desire to explore "dual identity and fantasy and reality and artifice versus realism" on the album, but then posed some thorny questions: "How can we become potentially the greatest part of ourselves by releasing our inhibitions in reference to fantasy? How can I reinvent myself, how can I remodel myself to become greater? How can I become more honest everyday?"

These are ambitious topics, no doubt, but Gaga was up for the challenge, as she was fired up by what she saw around her. *Born This Way* arrived at a pivotal time in American politics. Public support was growing for the legalization of same-sex marriage in the entire US, seven years after it was ruled legal in Massachusetts. In 2011, the US military also ended its controversial "Don't Ask, Don't Tell" policy, which cleared the way for members of the LGBTQIA+ community to enlist. Gaga, who identifies as bisexual, had long been supportive of gay rights, even driving eleven hours to Maine in 2010 to speak at a rally in support of the "Don't Ask, Don't Tell" repeal. (When the ban was finally lifted, Servicemembers United in Washington D.C.—an organization formed by veterans in support of the repeal—played her song "The Edge of Glory" at midnight in celebration.)

"I just have so much respect for my friends who live bisexual lives and who live transgender lives and who every single day have to fight for their identity and have to deal with all the things that come along with sexual orientation," she told *Huffington Post* in 2011. "I like to be as open but as diplomatic as I can be in order not to sensationalize bisexuality in pop music. I have no interest in using my sexual orientation to sell records."

Opposite *Flanked by designer and creative collaborator Nicola Formichetti (L) and bodyguard, Lady Gaga arrives at the Maxime Bar in Paris, France, on March 2, 2011*

Still, her being a member of the LGBTQIA+ community informs the power of the album's title track, which itself had roots in a classic gay anthem. "Born This Way" references a 1975 song by Valentino called "I Was Born This Way," which features a narrator who matter-of-factly says they're "happy, carefree and gay" and being this "ain't a fault—it's a fact." Two years later, an artist named Carl Bean covered the song while signed to Motown Records. Bean's version was a dance hit, peaking at No. 15 on *Billboard*'s Dance Club Songs chart the following year on the strength of a funky disco backbeat and his gospel-inspired vocals. A little over two decades later, Pour Homme—a.k.a. Stuart Price of Zoot Woman/Les Rythmes Digitales fame—sampled the song, while the Swedish pop artist Magnus Carlsson did a sleek pop-disco cover in 2008.

Gaga's propulsive 2011 version builds on the empowering sentiment of the original song, declaring, "It doesn't matter if you love him, or capital H-I-M" and stresses that people are born unique and special. From there, she assures groups typically bullied that they are perfect just the way they are, and Gaga herself fully supports them as they embrace their individuality. She wields clever turns of phrase ("Don't be a drag, just be a queen") and then calls out marginalized identities by name (e.g., Black people, people with disabilities, people who are gay, bi, lesbian, transgender) in a show of encouragement and solidarity. The end result is a skyscraping dance-floor filler that hit No. 1 in multiple countries and has since become a pride classic.

"When I put [the song 'Born This Way'] out, everybody was like, 'The lyrics are so literal,' and I'm like, 'Yeah,'" she said during an interview for Musicians@Google series. "When you get bullied, there's kind of an emotional poetry you go through in high school. 'Born This Way' is about saying, 'This is who I am. This is who the fuck I am.'" Bean—an activist and preacher who later founded and became the archbishop of the queer-friendly Unity Fellowship Church—praised Gaga's version to NPR in 2019. "I felt it was a great tribute, and it was the continuation of saving lives. So you know, it has just been a blessing to my life. And it's been a blessing, once again, to even another generation's life through the take that Gaga did on it."

The song's surging vibe set the tone for *Born This Way*. "Hair" links the freedom to switch up hairstyles to the idea of malleable identity—in fact, Gaga views changing hair as a reflection of the changing self—while "Judas" grapples with feeling torn between virtue and vice, in part by using Biblical references to Judas being deceptive and Jesus being betrayed three times, while "Government Hooker" is an extended metaphor for the ways the powers-that-be seduce and oppress. *Born This Way* also features plenty of empowered anthems: "Highway Unicorn (Road To Love)" is her version of the open-road dreamer anthems favored by her long-time musical obsession Bruce Springsteen, while "Marry the Night" encourages people to follow their dreams.

Fittingly, Gaga also invoked Springsteen to explain some of the album's we're-in-this-together vibe. "I related to Bruce because I watched my father, a blue collar American citizen, relate to Bruce and I think that in a social way, my fans feel blue collar," she told *Rolling Stone*. "They feel like they're the underdogs that will someday be the winners. And I took the influence of Bruce on my father in my life to create this album." Gaga also went right to the source—E Street Band saxophonist Clarence Clemons—to provide a thundering sax solo on "The Edge of Glory."

She envisioned the song as conjuring the Boss from a rhythmic perspective, although the lyrics were inspired by a different source: the moment when she said goodbye to her grandfather. "I got out a big thing of agave tequila and my dad sat next to me at the piano and we started doing shots back and forth," she said in an interview. "I wrote 'The Edge of Glory' on the piano and my dad and I cried. The song's about your last moment on Earth, the moment of truth, the edge of glory is that moment right before you leave the Earth."

"The Edge of Glory" embodies *Born This Way*'s maximalist approach to music: The song has a gigantic chorus, sledgehammer rhythms and stacks of interlocking keyboards. Gaga would characterize the album as "very hard and very edgy" in an interview with *The Sun*. "I would call it avant-garde techno rock," she said. "There's a lot of rock influences on the album, but not in a 'This is a rock music record' kind

of way. It actually is quite steadfast in that it is an exploration in electronic music and in techno sonics. But I have sort of created a genre of metal dance techno pop music with a lot of rock anthemic choruses because that is the music that I love."

She turned even more heads by calling out the "really big, almost big Def Leppard-style melodies in the choruses" on the album during *The Sun* interview. While her love of metal and hard rock was nothing new to fans, the mainstream music press was equal parts amused and impressed by her Def Leppard namedropping. Gaga was unfazed: For good measure, she worked with Robert John "Mutt" Lange—known for his meticulous, lacquered production on Def Leppard's smash records—on her song "Yoü and I," a song that also featured a cameo from Queen guitar god Brian May.

On the negative side, some criticized Gaga because "Born This Way" bore a striking resemblance to Madonna's 1989 hit "Express Yourself." The comparison's not that off base, especially in the chorus, though Gaga told Jay Leno during an appearance on *The Tonight Show with Jay Leno* there was no bad blood between the pop stars. "There is no one that is more adoring and a loving Madonna fan than me. I am the hugest fan personally and professionally. The good news is that I got

"I related to Bruce because I watched my father, a blue collar American citizen, relate to Bruce and I think that in a social way, my fans feel blue collar. And I took the influence of Bruce on my father in my life to create this album."
LADY GAGA

Opposite *Clarence Clemons (L) and Bruce Springsteen (R) of E Street Band. The band's music influenced Gaga's album* Born This Way, *with Clemons even playing sax solo on "The Edge of Glory."*

an email from her people and her sending me their love and complete support on behalf of the single. If the queen says it, it shall be." Madonna herself commented on the matter in a 2012 ABC interview, though her response wasn't quite as effusive: "When I heard ['Born This Way'] on the radio ... I said, 'That sounds very familiar.'" (To be fair, in the same interview, Madonna also called Gaga "a very talented artist" and complimented her songwriting.)

Born This Way became Gaga's first chart-topper in the US, selling a staggering 1.1 million copies during its first week in stores—just the seventeenth album to cross the million mark during its first seven days on sale. It helped that she appeared on *Saturday Night Live* again to promote the album. Not only did she look rather alien-like to perform "Born This Way," but she and host Justin Timberlake were in two sketches together, including with comedian Andy Samberg in the Lonely Island digital short for the throwback soul jam "3-Way (The Golden Rule)." In another boost, "The Edge of Glory" made the Top Ten of the *Billboard* charts the week *Born This Way* hit stores. Saxophonsit Clemons appeared in the song's video, which had a distinct 1980s vibe: Sporting a Cruella de Vil-style hairdo and some elaborate Versace outfits, Gaga cavorts in and around a New York City street and apartment, reclaiming the song as a way to embrace new beginnings.

In contrast, Gaga went grandiose and dug into an older wound—being dropped from her first record deal—as the plot device for the "Marry the Night" video. All of her clips to date were epics, but this particular mini-movie may have taken the cake for scope and ambition. The video starts with her in a hospital, feeling woozy and disoriented, before flashing back to her practicing ballet and receiving the fateful phone call about her lost deal. In this particular scene, she sports deep red lipstick and a black wig, and speaks French, giving the dramatic moment a cult noir feel. "It was one of the worst days of my life and it happened quite quickly, but in my mind, when I think back on that period of my life, it all happened very slow," she told NME of the day Island Def Jam dropped her. "[The video] is my personal way of seeing things."

And so in response to the devastating news, she dyes her hair and mutilates some clothing; in fact, a voiceover in the video declares, "I still had my bedazzler and I had a lot of patches, shiny ones from M&J Trimmings, so I wreaked havoc on some old denim." Next, a bedraggled Gaga escapes from a seedy street scene where cars burst into flames, and then starts rehearsing with other aspiring stars in a rigorous dance class. The video ends with a glimpse of her hand, on which is written "Interscope Records / Hollywood, CA / 4 p.m." As it turns out, she gets a happy ending.

Fashion-wise, Gaga's collaborators at the time echoed these hopeful, aspirational sentiments via outfits that challenged conventions. "At that time, there were a lot of things going on with regards to LGBTQ rights and female empowerment and all those things, and this album was really a starting point of taking back the ownership of our rights," collaborator and fashion director Nicola Formichetti told PAPER in 2021. "We wanted something very powerful—something strong and heroic and fearless, but with a Gaga twist. We wanted to do something that was about reality, but also fantasy at the same time. It was about creating looks that made a statement about living with no prejudice or judgment."

First and foremost was the *Born This Way* cover, which found Gaga's head welded to a motorcycle, looking like a Medusa hood ornament. "I think that cover was what really set the tone for the entire era," Formichetti says, "which was about the duality of real life and fantasy, and the two worlds colliding." For the "Judas" video, designer Alex Noble crafted a fringe-draped outfit made of dark-blue leather. MTV

News further described the clip as "an arty reimagining of the betrayal of Jesus Christ by Judas Iscariot," with Gaga portraying Mary Magdalene, and Christ and his apostles envisioned as a leather-clad motorcycle gang; actor Norman Reedus, meanwhile, plays Judas.

"I want to allow the video to speak for itself, but I will say that the theme of the video and the way that I wanted to aesthetically portray the story was as a motorcycle [Federico] Fellini movie, where the apostles are revolutionaries in a modern-day Jerusalem," she told the channel. "But it's meant more to celebrate faith than it is to challenge it."

The Catholic League once again condemned Gaga for this video, calling her "increasingly irrelevant" and adding, "She is trying to rip off Christian idolatry to shore up her talentless, mundane and boring performances." Gaga, meanwhile, told E! News she doesn't view the "Judas" video as "a religious statement. I view it as social statement. I view

Opposite *A Very Gaga Thanksgiving, 2011* **Above** *With then-fiancé Taylor Kinney in 2014. The pair first met in 2011 on the set of the music video for "Yoü And I," and split in 2016.*

Right *Lady Gaga as her alter-ego Jo Calderone (L) performs with Brian May (R) at the 2011 MTV Video Music Awards*

it as a cultural statement. It's a metaphor. It's not meant to be a Biblical lesson."

August brought the release of the "Yoü And I" video. Directed by Laurieann Gibson and filmed in Nebraska—the state where old flame Lüc Carl just happens to be from—the clip features various Gaga personas, including her as a mermaid. "The video is quite complex in the way that the story is told," she told MTV News, "and it's meant to be slightly linear and slightly twisted and confusing, which is the way that love is." Her cinematic journey was also difficult.

"I'm walking with no luggage and no nothing and it's just me and my ankles are bleeding a little bit and there's grass stuck in my shoes and I've got this outfit on and it's real sort of New York clothing and I'm sprinting," she explains. "And the [video is about the] idea that when you're away from someone you love, it's torture. I knew I wanted the video to be about me sprinting back and walking hundreds of thousands of miles to get him back."

Actor Taylor Kinney starred in the "Yoü And I" video—a fateful casting decision, as he and Gaga hit it off. "I remember I went up, and we're rolling, and I kissed her and she didn't expect it," he recalled on *Watch What Happens Live with Andy Cohen*. "They cut, and she slapped me. And then it was just awkward. And then the next take, I just did it again and then she didn't slap me. She didn't slap me then." She and Kinney started dating and later became engaged.

The cover of the "Yoü And I" single featured Gaga in drag, in the guise of her handsome alter-ego Jo Calderone, who had scruffy hair and sideburns and wore a white undershirt. Although people wouldn't think twice if Gaga did something like this today, critics back then didn't quite know what to do with Gaga's gender-bending. For example, ABC News ran the headline, "Lady Gaga as Jo Calderone: Brilliant or Creepy?" To Gaga, Jo Calderone was "meant to manipulate the visualization of gender in as many ways as I possibly could," she told *Huffington Post*. "And in a completely different way, sort of do that by creating what seems to be a straight man—a straight and quite relatable American man."

Left *Revving up the audience during the Born This Way Ball Asia tour in Taipei, Taiwan, May 18, 2012*

On August 28, Gaga performed "Yoü And I" with guest Brian May at the 2011 MTV Video Music Awards, immersed fully in her Jo Calderone persona. In fact, the appearance started with a chain-smoking Jo giving a lengthy monologue about Gaga that felt more like a comedic roast. "She's really fucking pissed at me," Gaga-as-Jo later told *Rolling Stone*, explaining why he was there instead. "Gaga said 'Fuck you,' she said, 'If you really love me you'll go instead of me and get in that spotlight.' So I did." Later, *Rolling Stone* asked Jo if he'd "hook up" with Britney Spears, drawing another coarse response. "Maybe if she wants to," he said. "She's fucking hot, Britney. Gaga's my girl, but Britney's fucking Britney Spears. Didn't you jerk off to Britney when you were a kid?"

In November, she starred in the TV special *A Very Gaga Thanksgiving*, which spawned the *A Very Gaga Holiday* EP, a four-song set that introduced Gaga's jazz side, highlighted by a languid "White Christmas" and an upbeat cover of "Orange Colored Sky." For the third year in a row, she was in contention for Album of the Year at the Grammy Awards, as *Born This Way* received a nomination. As it turns out, she also lost this category for the third year in a row—and was shut out of the other categories in which she was nominated.

In April 2012 she launched her next road trek, the Born This Way Ball. "The Haus of Gaga and I have worked for months conceiving a spectacular stage," Gaga said in a press release announcing the tour. Dubbing it an "electro-metal pop-opera," she described it as "the tale of the Beginning, the genesis of the Kingdom of Fame. How we were birthed and how we will die celebrating." In practice, that translated to an elaborate, gigantic stage set dominated by a haunted gothic castle—*Us Weekly* quoted an executive noting it's the "largest scenic structure that's ever been built to tour"—narrated by Mother G.O.A.T, or a distorted Gaga head in a computer-generated geometric shape. The tour also featured fashions created for her by Versace, Armani and Moschino ("It's been my life's dream to be dressed in Italian designers," Gaga told *Us Weekly*) and a general admission "Monster Pit" for dedicated fans.

Unfortunately, Gaga was forced to end the Born This Way Ball tour prematurely in February 2013 due to an injury. Although initial reports noted she had a labral tear in her hip, the injury was actually much more involved—and potentially career-derailing. "When we got all the MRIs finished before I went to surgery there were giant craters, a hole in my hip the size of a quarter, and the cartilage was just hanging out the other side of my hip," she told *Women's Wear Daily*. "I had a tear on the inside of my joint and a huge breakage." Had she not quit the tour when she did, she might have needed a full hip replacement. "I would have been out at least a year, maybe longer."

Even if she had been forced to take extended time off, *Born This Way*'s legacy was secure. The album wasn't just a stunning leap forward for Gaga—she also elevated the bar for pop music as a whole. "I want to be remembered for the message behind 'Born This Way,'" Gaga told *Vogue*. "I would like to be remembered for believing that people are equal. I would like to be remembered for being courageous and different."

Opposite and above *Gaga during her final show in Taiwan*

GRAMMY VESSEL

Lady Gaga was poised to have a big night at the 53rd Grammy Awards, which took place on February 13, 2011. For the second year in a row, she was up for Album of the Year—this time, for *The Fame Monster*—while "Dance In The Dark," "Telephone," and "Bad Romance" were all also nominated for awards. She ended up taking home three Grammys, but the gig was most memorable because of what she wore—or, rather, used as transportation.

Instead of strutting down the red carpet, she was carried down it in an egg-like vessel, by a team that included several muscular shirtless men. The contraption was designed by Hussein Chalayan, the same visionary behind her high-concept bubble dress. Chalayan had constructed a similar vessel for his 2003 movie called *Place to Passage*; Gaga's luxe transportation reportedly took more than a month to build.

She remained in the vessel through her performance of "Born This Way" during the show. The egg glowed slightly as it was wheeled onstage and then opened to reveal Gaga, who "hatched" out of it and immediately put on a flat-brimmed hat. Later, Gaga told radio host Ryan Seacrest she spent seventy-two hours in the plexiglass egg—which was temperature-controlled—leading up to the performance. "It was a very creative experience," she said. "It was time for me to really prepare and think about the meaning of the song and get prepared for the performance."

Living in an enclosed space for days on end is certainly a nod to her background in method acting—but also pointed to her single-minded artistic vision. "I really wanted to be born onstage," she told Seacrest. "The creative vessel was helpful for me to stay focused. We had it backstage so that I was able to really stay in this sort of creative, embryonic incubation."

Fittingly, she wore a flesh-colored latex outfit designed by Thierry Mugler X Perry Meek for her "Born This Way" performance, comprising a crop top, a clingy long skirt and coat, and boots. Very subtly, she also boasted some realistic-looking prosthetics on her skin, giving her sharp, almost squared-off shoulders. To accept her Grammy for Best Pop Vocal Album, she wore another wild Thierry Mugler outfit: a black rubber dress "inspired by humanoids ... alien sex humanoid hybrid woman," Gaga told Jay Leno. Accordingly, the outfit boasted extra padding at the bust and butt, giving her an otherworldly vibe.

"I really wanted to be born onstage. We had the egg backstage so that I was able to really stay in this sort of creative, embryonic incubation." LADY GAGA

Above and opposite *Lady Gaga emerges from an egg-like vessel designed by Hussein Chalayan, to be born onstage at the 53rd Annual Grammy Awards*

GIVING BACK

Previous spread *Lady Gaga joins his Holiness the Dalai Lama (L) to speak to US mayors about kindness, June 26, 2016, in Indianapolis, Indiana*

Opposite *Lady Gaga's mom, Cynthia Germanotta, who serves as president of the Born This Way Foundation*

"We always talked about doing something together, giving back. It wasn't so much a 'decision' as something we always wanted to do."
CYNTHIA GERMANOTTA

Born This Way wasn't just a musical turning point for Lady Gaga. During this era, she used her newfound superstar platform to try and make the world a better place. Speaking candidly to *The Metro* newspaper, Gaga detailed the things that meant the most to her heart, including being close to her family and fans.

"I'm in tune with what [the fans] want. And I'm in tune with myself, too. At the end of the day, I have to look myself in the mirror and I'm proud of everything I stand for. I have no reason to do or say anything unless it comes from my soul." After noting she works hard and eschews partying ("You don't see me falling out of nightclubs and buying Range Rovers"), she crystallized her vision: "Social justice and music are the two most paramount things in my life and I can't put it more plainly."

Accordingly, it makes perfect sense that Gaga would find a way to combine these two passions into something that would change the world—and she would do this life-changing work with her beloved mom. "We always talked about doing something together, giving back," Cynthia Germanotta told *The Daily Beast*. "As my daughter's career took off, we started having more serious conversations about it. It wasn't so much a 'decision' as something we always wanted to do."

Their joint endeavor is a nonprofit called the Born This Way Foundation. "To be able to build it with our daughter and my family has been very rewarding, but it actually came out of some struggles," Germanotta told *InStyle* in 2018, adding that the organization arose from Gaga's "passion and her desire to help young people be better equipped than she felt that she was to deal with her problems."

Although Gaga had mentioned this cruelty before, launching the Born This Way Foundation brought more traumatic stories to light. Cynthia recalled one particularly egregious high school incident where Gaga's classmates planned a party and deliberately didn't invite the teenager—

but, on the following Monday, pointedly asked what she did over the weekend. In 2012, Gaga revealed to the *New York Times* that neighborhood boys also once tossed her in a trash can—a staggering assault that stuck with her for years.

"I was called really horrible, profane names very loudly in front of huge crowds of people, and my schoolwork suffered at one point," Gaga said. "I didn't want to go to class. And I was a straight-A student, so there was a certain point in my high school years where I just couldn't even focus on class because I was so embarrassed all the time. I was so ashamed of who I was."

Cynthia told *InStyle* that this bullying had a profound impact on Gaga. "It shattered her self-value, her sense of self worth, and she began to develop anxiety and depression in middle school. It's something that followed her through college and even through her career." (A former NYU classmate of Gaga's recalled seeing a Facebook group dedicated to mocking the aspiring performer.)

Above *(L-R) Chelsea Clinton, Lady Gaga, and Cynthia Germanotta at the Z100 Pride Live Stonewall Day concert in New York, on June 28, 2019*

"I am now a woman, I have a voice in the universe, and I want to do everything I can to become an expert in social justice and hope I can make a difference and mobilize young people to change the world."
LADY GAGA

However, the Born This Way Foundation wasn't formed specifically to combat bullying. Instead, Gaga and her mom (who serves as the organization's president) have long stressed it's geared toward promoting and encouraging kindness, "I believe it is more important than ever to motivate an agenda of kindness," she explained to the *New York Times*. "Kindness that leads to the healing of the mind, body, and soul. Kindness that invigorates programs that are fearless in their effort to help humanity learn the importance of self-care."

In February 2012, Gaga officially unveiled the Born This Way Foundation at Harvard University. "The culture of love is not going to change overnight but youth are the answer to creating a braver, kinder world," she said at the launch event. "This might be one of the best days of my life." The Born This Way Foundation was not "restitution or revenge for my experiences," Gaga stressed to the *New York Times*. "I want to make that clear. This is: I am now a woman, I have a voice in the universe, and I want to do everything I can to become an expert in social justice and hope I can make a difference and mobilize young people to change the world."

Today, the Born This Way Foundation develops programs and community resources, conducts research, and provides resources to help youths succeed. Gaga too remains deeply involved with the foundation. For example, she uses the website to open up conversations about mental health. In 2016, she revealed a diagnosis of post-traumatic stress disorder (PTSD) as a result of several things, including being raped by an older producer, an assault she had started discussing only a few years before. After her disclosure, she published an open letter on the foundation's website explaining her situation. "There is a lot of shame attached to mental illness, but it's important that you know that there is hope and a chance for recovery," she wrote, as part of a letter that made it clear pop superstardom doesn't insulate people from pain.

"[I] struggle with triggers from the memories I carry from my feelings of past years on tour when my needs and requests for balance were being ignored," she wrote. "I was overworked and not taken seriously when I shared my pain and concern that something was wrong." She shared that being injured on the Born This Way Ball tour permanently changed her: "The experience of performing night after night in mental and physical pain ingrained in me a trauma that I relive when I see or hear things that remind me of those days."

This willingness to be so open and honest underscores her unique career approach. "I did not get into this business for the money," she told *American Idol* host Ryan Seacrest in 2011, during an appearance on his radio show. "I don't care about the material things. I don't do this because I want tons of attention. I did it because it was my destiny to be a performer and to be part of mobilising the voice of my generation."

While that's certainly a lofty statement, kindness is one area that Gaga takes incredibly seriously. It's the one constant

in a music career marked by reinvention and change. "As my career has grown and changed and I've done different things, I've become very mindful of my position in the world and my responsibility to humanity and to those who follow me," she told Oprah Winfrey during a 2019 interview for *Elle*. "And I consider myself to be a kindness punk."

Although that might seem like a contradiction—as a genre, punk is known for being aggressive and sometimes angry—she has a very logical explanation. "Punks have a sort of reputation for being rebellious, right?" she continued. "So for me, I really view my career, and even what I'm doing now, as a rebellion against all the things in the world that I see to be unkind. Kindness heals the world. Kindness heals people. It's what brings us together—it's what keeps us healthy."

Above *The Born Brave Bus; an interactive traveling experience where fans could learn more about the Born This Way Foundation*
Opposite *Lady Gaga presents her mom with the Global Changemakers award at the 10th Annual Children Mending Hearts Empathy Rocks fundraiser, June 10, 2018, Los Angeles, California*

Award

7

ARTPOP

Previous spread *In Japan promoting* ARTPOP, *December 1, 2013*

Opposite *Lady Gaga in a habit-like robe opens the 2013 MTV Video Music Awards, August 25, 2013, in New York City*

"When I wrote *Born This Way*, I demonstrated a sense of maturity. And I feel that, on the next album, there's a lack of maturity, it's a tremendous lack of maturity or sense of responsibility."
LADY GAGA

Many artists who have successful debut albums struggle when making album number two. They've spent their whole lives amassing material for their first effort, and then have a finite amount of time to come up with more brilliance for the follow-up. If you've ever heard of the sophomore slump—it's very real, and can be creatively destabilizing.

Ever the overachiever, Lady Gaga didn't hit a commercial stumbling block until her third album, ARTPOP. Although it became her second album to top the *Billboard* 200, its first-week numbers—258,000 copies—paled in comparison to the blockbuster, million-plus-selling *Born This Way*. Overall, ARTPOP only produced two hit singles, "Applause" and "Do What U Want," and polarized critics.

Part of this tepid response had to do with familiarity; lyrically, Gaga seemed to be drawing from the same themes as previous efforts. "It's my intention for you to have a really good time," Gaga told L.A. radio station KIIS-FM. "I designed it for it to be fun from start to finish, like a night at the club in terms of the DJing aspect of it. When you listen to it, it really flows nicely. It's really fun to pop in with your friends. I really wrote it for me and my friends to pop in from start to finish." Paradoxically, pop artists had started trying to mimic Gaga's empowerment vibe and obsession with fame, but overlooked her Warholian celebrity critiques. In other words, she had created a, well, monster: a movement of fame-obsessed pop stars who succeeded at being inspirational, but didn't create music with much depth.

To be fair, Gaga herself was also trying to dial back the seriousness of her music on ARTPOP. "Let's just say, I feel that when I wrote *Born This Way*, I demonstrated a sense of maturity," she told an Australian crowd in July 2012. "And I feel that, on the next album, there's a lack of maturity, it's a tremendous lack of maturity or sense of responsibility." Fittingly, Gaga ushered in the ARTPOP era with that

common act of rebellion, a cryptic tattoo. "New ink, new album," she tweeted in August 2012, along with a photo of the word "ARTPOP" neatly inked on her arm. In another tweet, she revealed the ink was the album's name: "Make sure when writing about my new album/project ARTPOP that you CAPITALIZE the title, it's all in the details." The phrase and its all-caps rendering signaled Gaga was going for something different.

ARTPOP's cover—a realistic sculpture of a naked Gaga cupping her breasts, with a giant blue orb in front of her called a gazing ball—unpacked some of this mysterious meaning. Jeff Koons, the artist responsible for the sculpture and the album's artwork, told MTV News the gazing ball "really does become kind of the symbol for everything—and this aspect of reflection that when you come across something like a gazing ball, it affirms you, it affirms your existence and then from that affirmation, you start to want more," he says. "There's a transcendence that takes place

Above and opposite *Lady Gaga invokes Botticelli's* Birth of Venus *during her performance at the 2013 MTV Video Music Awards*

and eventually it really leads you to everything." To add more depth, he added kaleidoscopic fragments of Gian Lorenzo Bernini's *Apollo and Daphne* and Botticelli's *Birth of Venus* behind her on the album artwork.

ARTPOP's first single, "Applause," arrived on August 12, 2013, a week ahead of the scheduled date due to snippets of the song being leaked online. As with the other singles she released to preview albums, the song is bold and brash, with slamming beats, an explosive chorus and passionate vocals. "I believe in show business," she tweeted after the song's release. "The 'Applause' is what breeds that thing that I love. When I know I've made you happy. When I know it was good." The messaging was a subtle shift from her previous songs about fame: The narrator needs that applause for validation, whereas before they might analyze the folly of craving such positive reinforcement. That's not necessarily cynical, however: Producer DJ White Shadow told MTV News that Gaga "has a complete and total adoration for her fans. I've never seen anyone in my entire life work as hard or do as much for her fans. It's a back-and-forth thing. She does so much for them that they naturally want to do stuff for her."

The accompanying music video was directed by fashion photographer duo Inez and Vinoodh, and was "inspired by the entertainer's passion for shapeshifting," Gaga tweeted. "Would you do 'anything' for the applause? Iconography in motion, as magic." Appropriately, she switches outfits at a dizzying pace—a black full-body leotard with a head covering, a bra made from gloved hands, a green jacket comprised of what looks like tiny tiles—and references an impressive amount of great works of art. A writer for *Out* saw parallels with Warhol's Marilyn Monroe paintings when Gaga pairs a striking yellow wig and red lipstick with black-and-white photo tinting, and Fritz Lang's *Metropolis* in certain costumes and poses, including a pyramid. At another surreal point, her head is grafted on to the body of a swan.

The following week, Gaga opened the 2013 MTV Video Music Awards with a typically elaborate performance that referenced the video. She started off wearing a bulky white robe that looked vaguely like a nun's habit, before having it torn off to reveal a sleek black bodysuit and stockings. From there, dancers helped her take off and put on various articles of clothing (a sparkly royal blue coat and matching skirt) and wigs (a mustard-yellow mop) before she disappeared and ended the song with a big wardrobe reveal: a shell bra and bikini bottom. The outfit represented the birth of Gaga-as-Venus—and ushered in ARTPOP. By early September, the song peaked at No. 4 on the *Billboard* Hot 100.

Above *With DJ White Shadow (L) at "artRave" on November 10, 2013, in New York City*

"[Gaga] has a complete and total adoration for her fans. I've never seen anyone in my entire life work as hard or do as much for her fans."
DJ WHITE SHADOW

On *ARTPOP*, Gaga once again worked with DJ White Shadow, who was instrumental in the sound of *Born This Way*, and co-wrote a song with RedOne. However, she also teamed up with dance world A-listers—including Zedd, David Guetta, Infected Mushroom, and Madeon—enlisted Whitesnake/ Dio guitarist Doug Aldrich and production whiz will.i.am, and collaborated with rappers Too Short, Twista, and T.I. This ensured *ARTPOP*'s sound was far different from her previous efforts, even the remix albums.

While nominally a mainstream dance effort with booming beats, stacked production and Gaga's typically formidable vocals, *ARTPOP* most often feels like an underground electro-pop art project. "Swine" is industrial-metal with an EDM heart; the piano-freckled "Fashion!" has the precision and theatrical glamour of Bowie's 1980 hit; "Aura" is zippered-up robot-rock with the *savoir faire* of Daft Punk.

The album's minimalist title track is even more intriguing. A de facto mission statement, it's about as confessional as Gaga gets. She admits she isn't great at being insincere or overtly self-promotional, because she's always motivated by music, not fancy things or shiny baubles. However, "Artpop" also imparts some hard-won wisdom about the importance of being resilient and staying optimistic, even (and especially) when things feel dark and hopeless. In fact, Gaga encourages people to embrace the power of music, as creativity can be a form of self-care and solace—if not personal redemption. Her vocals sometimes sound disfigured on verses, though the chorus ("We could belong together, ARTPOP") are solemn and clear as a bell. Speaking to SiriusXM satellite radio, she described the song somewhat cryptically as "an inferno, and it's the only song on the record that I didn't really want it to go anywhere or explode or orgasm, because in a way that would be like composing something that's just like every other orgasm I've ever had."

From more Gaga comments on SiriusXM, many of *ARTPOP*'s songs are obsessed with sex, including "MANiCURE" ("This song is about getting ready to go out and catch a man or catch a girl to fool around with"), "Sexxx Dreams" (self-explanatory), and "Venus" (a song about "sex in the most mythological way"). However, *ARTPOP* could also have a sense of humor. The interstellar lust displayed by the narrator of "Venus" doubles as being drunk on fame ("Uranus, don't you know my ass is famous?" she screeches), while the spelling of "MANiCURE" is deliberately meant to convey ambiguity: She pronounces the word like "man-cured," as if someone is being rescued by a guy.

Yet she revealed that "Dope" is about her becoming addicted to marijuana, and "G.U.Y." is about subverting

expectations. "What I really like about 'G.U.Y.' is that it's about third-wave feminism, which is that we don't feel the need to be on top all the time or be in charge or take control like a man," she explained. "I'm a power bottom, I like to be underneath."

The biggest misstep on *ARTPOP* is "Jewels N' Drugs," the collaboration with T.I., Twista, and Too Short, as rap and hip-hop aren't Gaga's strongest suits. More controversial was "Do What U Want," which featured rapper R. Kelly. The song itself was overtly sexual, as Gaga sang lines such as "Do what you want with my body" atop propulsive techno-pop music. However, at the time of the song's release, Kelly was five years removed from being found not guilty on charges he filmed himself having sex with an underage girl. That fact came up in a 2013 Japanese press conference, to which Gaga replied, "R. Kelly and I have sometimes had very untrue things written about us, so in a way this was a bond between us. That we were able to say, 'The public, they can have our bodies, but they cannot have our mind or our heart.' It was a really natural collaboration." A video filmed for the song was also never released, though "Do What U Want" reached No. 13 on the *Billboard* singles chart.

Years later, after the release of the documentary *Surviving R. Kelly*, which featured multiple women detailing abuse by the rapper, Gaga apologized "for my poor judgment when I was young and for not speaking out sooner" and issued a statement. "I stand behind these women 1000%, believe

Above *Arriving at the YouTube Music Awards 2013 sporting a bizarre look, even by Gaga's standards*

them, know they are suffering and in pain, and feel strongly that their voices should be heard and taken seriously. As a victim of sexual assault myself, I made both the song and the video at a dark time in my life. My intention was to create something extremely defiant and provocative because I was angry and still hadn't processed the trauma that had occurred in my own life." Gaga subsequently removed the song from streaming services and future physical pressings of *ARTPOP*.

This situation wasn't the only hint of discord. On November 3, she made an auspicious appearance at the YouTube Music Awards. Her red carpet look—sunglasses, a hat and grimy prosthetic teeth—was something straight out of *Tim Burton's The Nightmare Before Christmas*. However, her performance for the new song "Dope" was worrying: Sporting a baseball hat and boxy flannel shirt, she cried at the start of the song while apologizing to her mom, and never quite recovered. The *Los Angeles Times* dubbed the performance "deeply strange and out-of-tune," and in hindsight it was a clear sign things were amiss.

This appearance was followed up by an elaborate and over-the-top (even for Gaga) two-day album release party extravaganza, ArtRave, at a warehouse in Brooklyn, New York. The space featured art from Jeff Koons—the realistic sculpture of a naked Gaga holding a giant blue orb was prominently on display, alongside four other sculptures—as well as Gaga videos lensed by Marina Abramović, and contortionists.

Above *Demonstrating the world's first flying dress, Volantis, 2013*

Left *Lady Gaga rides the red carpet sidesaddle on a giant white "horse" as she arrives for the 2013 American Music Awards*

Opposite Lady Gaga & The Muppets' Holiday Spectacular, 2013

Following spread *Looking spectacular on the first night of the UK leg of ArtRave: The* ARTPOP *Ball tour, on October 15, 2014*

At ArtRave, she also announced her intention of performing in outer space in 2015. "I want to make a moment that is about much more than me," she later told *Harper's Bazaar*. "Performing in space is such an honor. I want to challenge myself to come up with something that will not only bring everyone together but will also have a message of love that blasts into the beyond." Additionally, Gaga debuted Volantis, which she classified as "the world's first flying dress" and "a purpose-designed transport prototype designed to carry one person in a controlled hover and directional movement." (In reality, while wearing Volantis she appeared to be standing under a giant Ikea lamp with multiple bulbs.) According to a *Pitchfork* review, Volantis's first flight wasn't a rousing success: "It roared to life and lurched forward a few feet, hovering. Then it did the same thing, backwards. Then it stopped. That was it. Never before have I felt more like I was living a scene from *Spinal Tap*."

It was an auspicious sign, as critics were also hot and cold on *ARTPOP*'s music. *Billboard* raved, saying Gaga "offered fans her most sonically and lyrically diverse album to date" and *Exclaim!* dubbed it a "dynamic, memorable album" that "reveals a performer who finally sounds as invested in her art

as she is in her image." However, *Entertainment Weekly* was split: "As pop, the album is a well-executed and entertaining tour of Gaga's tried-and-true tricks. But as art, it falls short when it comes to one basic function: making an impression." *AllMusic*, meanwhile, noted "ARTPOP never insinuates or settles in the subconscious; it always assaults, determined to make an impression even when all it has to say is that it doesn't have much to say." And the blog *The Line of Best Fit* says the album "lacks the key component that made the bizarre spectacles that accompanied her other albums slightly less irritating: consistently good pop songs."

Gaga nevertheless pressed on with elaborate promotion. She pulled double duty as host and musical guest on *Saturday Night Live*, and held her own throughout the night's skits. Looking like Donatella Versace with long, straight blonde hair and a pale purple dress, Gaga rode down the 2013 American Music Awards red carpet astride a gorgeous white "horse"—which was, in reality, two people crouched down acting like the animal. Around Thanksgiving, she did the throwback primetime variety show, *Lady Gaga & The Muppets' Holiday Spectacular*, which featured guest stars such as RuPaul, Kristen Bell, and Joseph Gordon-Levitt.

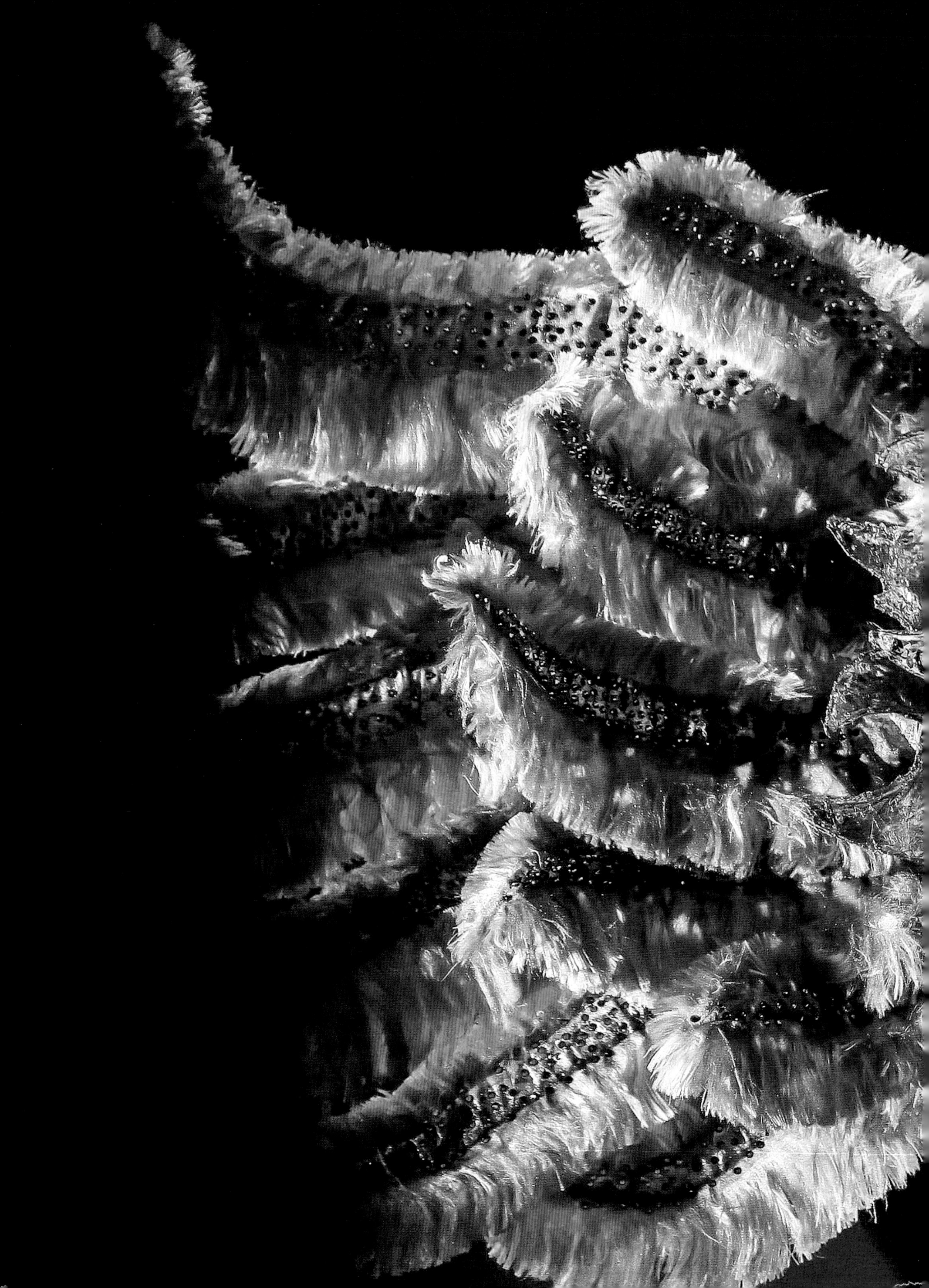

Elton John also joined Gaga on the show for a performance of his 1974, No. 1 hit "Bennie and the Jets" (which he playfully renamed to "Gaga and the Jets") and the *ARTPOP* title track.

Her friendship with John, which kicked off in earnest with the pair's 2010 Grammys performance, would prove to be a grounding presence for her during this turbulent time. In February 2011, he and Gaga recorded a duet, "Hello, Hello," for the movie *Gnomeo & Juliet*. It ended up being nominated for Best Original Song at the Golden Globe Awards and Best Song at the Critics' Choice Movie Awards, as well as Best Original Song at the Satellite Awards. A few months later, John and his husband, David Furnish, named Gaga the godmother of their son, Zachary Jackson Levon Furnish-John. The decision was as much pragmatic as it was personal, John said. "Zachary's going to inherit an incredible musical legacy from his father one day, and she will be a good person to guide him through the ins and outs of the music business, 'cause she sure knows everything about the business now," he said at the time. Fittingly, Gaga crooned "Somewhere Over the Rainbow" to him early on. In early 2013, Gaga would also become godmother to the couple's next son, Elijah Joseph Daniel Furnish-John.

However, as the album campaign progressed, it became clear that behind-the-scenes professional turmoil was taking a toll—specifically, the fact that she and her long-time

Below *A disturbing performance at the South by Southwest Music Festival in 2014 includes performance artist Millie Brown force vomiting on Gaga*

manager Troy Carter parted ways a week before *ARTPOP* came out. While some industry publications credited the split to the diplomatic (if vague) "creative differences," the *New York Times* reported that Gaga fired Carter.

The extent of this conflict became clearer in the months after *ARTPOP*'s release. In January 2014, when the video for "Do What U Want" was initially only delayed, not cancelled, Gaga took to her Little Monsters social networking site and noted she was only given a week "to plan and execute" the clip. She then blamed some unnamed people around her. "Those who have betrayed me gravely mismanaged my time and health and left me on my own to damage control any problems that ensued as a result."

Gaga went on to allege that after her tour-ending February 2013 surgery, she was left to fend for herself. "After my surgery, I was too sick, too tired and too sad to control the damage on my own," she wrote. "My label was not aware that this was going on." She added that "those who did not care about *ARTPOP*'s success are now gone ... I never thought after all the years of hard work that those I called friends and partners would ever care so little at a time I needed them the most."

More worrying were parts of a one-off March 2014 concert inside a gigantic Doritos vending machine located at the South by Southwest (SXSW) music festival. The festival always possesses a slightly unhinged, spring break-

Below *Lady Gaga helps send off the legendary New York City venue Roseland Ballroom with a live show on March 28, 2014*

like atmosphere; Gaga's performance was no exception. During a thrashing, electro-rock version of "Swine," she sat down behind a set of drums and screamed until her voice was raw. As the song progressed, an artist named Millie Brown who was known for her performative vomiting (really) stuck her fingers down her throat and threw up a bright-green liquid all over Gaga. Later, the pair ended up balanced on a gyrating pig with an apple in its mouth; Brown once again force-vomited on Gaga, who was lying down screaming, "Fuck you, pop music! This is ARTPOP! Free yourself!"

Pop star Demi Lovato very quickly accused the performance of "glamorizing" eating disorders, though Brown pushed back on that notion. "I can understand why people would make that association, but my performance really is not a statement about eating disorders themselves," she told MTV News. "It's like using my body to express

Opposite *Lady Gaga brings ArtRave: The ARTPOP Ball tour to Madison Square Garden in New York City, on May 13, 2014* **Above** *Onstage at Staples Center on July 21, 2014, in Los Angeles, California*

Left *Lady Gaga (Center) poses "Paws up!" with her dancers, 2014*

This Little
Fan
gaga

Opposite *Singing "Paparazzi" while reclining in a crystal hand shaped into Gaga's "Paws up!" sign, in Pittsburgh on May 8, 2014*

myself. I think a lot of people understand that I'm not trying to punish myself and my body in that way." Gaga also felt compelled to step in and clarify their intentions with the song. "Millie and I know that not everybody's going to love that performance, but we both really believe in artistic expression and strong identities, and I support her and what she does," she told *TODAY*. "*ARTPOP*, my new album, is about bringing art and music together in the spirit of creative rebellion, and for us, that performance was art in its purest form."

Gaga was in this kind of defensive position for much of the *ARTPOP* era, which had to be difficult. Months after the album's release, Gaga was clearly still processing the split with her management and how it affected the album. When asked by the *Associated Press* in September 2014 if "disagreements with management" had an impact on *ARTPOP*'s genesis, she responded, "I would have to say that whole situation had less to do with creativity differences and more to do with me really needing some time from myself to be creative." She then cited a "schedule [that] was way too difficult" that was driven by misguided priorities. "I was not able to keep up and my whole business became very focused on making as much money as possible as quickly as possible, which is really not where my heart is. My integrity as a musician is so much more important to me than money."

As these conversations reveal, the *ARTPOP* era was distinguished by some of Gaga's most candid, personal interviews yet. In a December 2014 appearance on *The Howard Stern Show*, she clarified that the SXSW performance of "Swine" alluded to the fact a man "could never, ever degrade me as much as I degrade myself" and revealed she was raped by an older producer as a "very naive" nineteen-year-old. In fact, the song "Swine" itself is "about rape," she added. "The song is about demoralization. The song is about rage and fury and passion, and I had a lot of pain that I wanted to release." Later in the Howard Stern interview, she noted that she didn't "want to be defined" by the assault, and flashed her usual defiance. "I'll be damned if somebody's gonna say that every creatively intelligent thing that I ever did is all boiled down to one dickhead who did that to me."

She discussed her bisexuality in frank and open terms on a separate appearance on Andy Cohen's *Watch What Happens Live*. "I've taken a few dips in the lady pond. I like girls," she said. "I know people think I just say things to be shocking, but I actually do like pussy. It just depends on whose pussy it is. For me, it's similar to how I feel about guys. It's more of an energy thing." She added that she used to enjoy frequenting lesbian clubs ("I find lesbians to be way more daring than straight men, when it comes to coming on to you. And I really like that") and noted that "it wasn't until I found a guy that could come on to me as strong as a lesbian"—meaning her then-boyfriend, Taylor Kinney—"that I fell in love."

In the *ARTPOP* era, Gaga also experienced the kind of backlash pop stars often receive—the kind that comes after sustained success—and was forced to defend herself after making bold statements. "You know what? It's not a lie that I am bisexual and I like women," she said during a promotional stop. Anyone that wants to twist this into 'She says she's bisexual for marketing,' this is a fucking lie. This is who I am and who I have always been."

Gaga took the musical critiques more in stride, telling the *Associated Press* in later 2014, "I'm actually very proud of *ARTPOP*. As much as it's had a lot of criticism, I think a lot of that had to with where I am in my career, I've been on top for a long time, I think it's the nature of this industry—we love to build them up to tear them down." Getting to this sanguine place no doubt took a lot of time, conversation and personal reflection. "I went through a rough time last year," she told *Harper's Bazaar*. "I felt very taken advantage of by people I trusted. I asked my mother, 'I work so hard. I never stop. I never say no. Why doesn't this person love me, Mom? Why was this person willing to hurt me to help themselves? Why wasn't I enough? Why is money more important than me?'"

She said that her mom "reminded me to forgive others for not seeing God where I see it," and added, "I see God in my fans. She said, 'You're hurt because you don't operate this way. You are fiercely protective of your inventions because you are your fans.' She helped me understand my own feelings. When someone has pulled the wool over my eyes, I feel that they have pulled the wool over the eyes of millions of fans around the world. She helped me to forgive. You can't force people to have the same world consciousness and awareness as you do."

As usual, Gaga's solace was a place where like-minded people gathered: her shows. In late March and early April, she played a string of shows to send off the legendary New York City venue Roseland Ballroom. The following month, she launched artRave: The ARTPOP Ball. The tour's design certainly had her usual escapism vibe: In a nod to the "rave" designation, colorful lights and effects were used throughout, giving the stage a warehouse dance-party vibe. However, the show didn't neglect real life concerns; she read heartbreaking fan mail during the show and brought people onstage to sit with her during "Born This Way."

"When I'm onstage with the *ARTPOP* Ball, the point of the show is to take what was the mess of my life and make art of it," she told *The Independent*. "To raise the spirit of artistic dreams and creativity and take all the things I was feeling in pain about, and rage ... I take a much more meditative approach to the performance. I've got wide-open ears. The ArtRave has routines, and there's a performance-art aspect that has been designed."

Her outfits nod to this, and included a get-up that looked like a Strawberry Shortcake character going raving; a white leotard with black polka dots and removable accents shaped into tentacles, making it appear she's being hugged by an octopus; and a silvery-white Versace dress that resembled a *Jetsons* costume. She also played some otherworldly instruments—a jaw-dropping custom keytar shaped like a seahorse and a piano built into replicas of jagged ice pieces—and sang "Paparazzi" sitting in a crystal hand with long pink nails that was bent into her "Paws up!" sign.

As Gaga's tour continued, the courts also finally resolved one aspect of her early career. In late 2014, Wendy Starland triumphed in her lawsuit against Rob Fusari and his company, winning more than $7.3 million, and half of whatever Gaga pays him in the future. During the long, drawn-out court case, Gaga testified in support of her friend. "My understanding was that Wendy and him had initially agreed upon 50/50 perhaps before Wendy ever found me, and after I was signed to Rob and made music, Rob began to change his mind," she said in a deposition quoted by *Billboard*.

"Making this album was like heart surgery, I was desperate, in pain, and poured my heart into electronic music that slammed harder than any drug I could find."

LADY GAGA

By the end of 2014, she was in a better headspace, making plans for future music and able to have perspective on the fact she was depressed at the end of 2013. "Depression doesn't take away your talents—it just makes them harder to find," she told *Harper's Bazaar*. "But I always find it. I learned that my sadness never destroyed what was great about me. You just have to go back to that greatness, find that one little light that's left. I'm lucky I found one little glimmer stored away."

That glimmer ended up burning bright for years to come. After being misunderstood upon release, *ARTPOP* has become something of a cult classic, redeemed by fans and the passage of time. In April 2021, fans started a viral Twitter campaign to push people to buy the album, in hopes of bringing about a sequel. The push significantly moved the needle around the globe, and *ARTPOP* returned to the iTunes digital sales charts.

"The petition to #buyARTPOPoniTunes for a volume II has inspired such a tremendous warmth in my heart," Gaga tweeted. "Making this album was like heart surgery, I was desperate, in pain, and poured my heart into electronic music that slammed harder than any drug I could find." After tweeting three hearts and celebratory hand emojis, she added, "I fell apart after I released this album. Thank you for celebrating something that once felt like destruction. We always believed it was ahead of its time. Years later turns out, sometimes, artists know. And so do little monsters. Paws up."

Opposite *Lady Gaga paints her face to mimic the cover of her single "Applause"*

CHEEK TO CHEEK

Previous spread *Tony Bennett (L) and Lady Gaga (R): Cheek To Cheek Live!, 2014*

Opposite *Lady Gaga and Tony Bennett onstage at Umbria Jazz at the Arena Santa Giuliana, Italy, July 15, 2015*

Lady Gaga and Tony Bennett might not seem to have much in common. He's a senior citizen jazz crooner; she's a metal-loving pop singer millennial. However, both artists are incredibly versatile—Bennett had massive pop success decades before Gaga was born, including with 1962's "I Left My Heart in San Francisco"—and both are prone to reinvention. For example, Bennett is also a decorated painter and he performed on MTV *Unplugged* in the nineties with artists such as Elvis Costello and k.d. lang. Still, Gaga's pivot from scrappy performance artist to sophisticated jazz chanteuse is one of music's great unexpected evolutions. That her collaborations with Bennett worked so well—and sounded so natural—is also a marvel.

The pair first crossed paths in 2011 at a Robin Hood Foundation benefit gala where Gaga performed. Bennett was particularly wowed by the pop star's take on Nat King Cole's "Orange Colored Sky" and asked to meet her. "I said, 'Oh, my gosh, Tony Bennett's here,'" Gaga told *Rolling Stone* in 2014. "And I was so nervous. I fixed my hair, and my mom was fixing her makeup. We went back to meet him, and he said, 'Do you want to do a jazz album together?' I said, 'Yes, of course I do.' And we were fast friends and friends ever since." Gaga became so fond of him, in fact, she got a tattoo of a Bennett sketch of a trumpet in June 2014.

The proposed full-length album took some time to coalesce, as Gaga was laid up recovering from her *Born This Way* tour injuries. However, the pair knew their collaboration was going to work, as they tracked a peppy, playful take on Rodgers and Hart's "The Lady Is a Tramp" for Bennett's 2011 album, *Duets II*. The crooner couldn't say enough good things about Gaga at the time, praising her singing, dancing, and piano skills. "She came in so prepared and so knowledgeable about what to do," Bennett told *Rolling Stone*. "She's as good as Ella Fitzgerald or anybody you want to come up with … She's very strong. I know it sounds way out, but she could become

"She's as good as Ella Fitzgerald or anybody you want to come up with … she could become America's Picasso if they leave her alone."
TONY BENNETT

AZIOLI

Opposite *Lady Gaga plays piano at a Robin Hood Foundation benefit gala in New York, 2011: a performance that wowed Tony Bennett*

Above *Lady Gaga shows off her trumpet tattoo designed by Tony Bennett, August 3, 2016*

America's Picasso if they leave her alone and let her just do what she has to do. She is very, very talented."

Three years later, when Gaga and Bennett taped a concert for the PBS show *Great Performances*, he echoed these sentiments. Walking the red carpet before the show, which took place at the Jazz at Lincoln Center's Rose Theater, Bennett told *Rolling Stone* that their joint album would feature "all the great songs" by composers such as George Gershwin, Cole Porter and Irving Berlin. "No other country has ever given the rest of the world so many magnificent songs, and they're gonna live forever. Wait 'til you find out when she sings those songs." However, Bennett also stressed that it wasn't *what* Gaga sang—but *how* she sang it—that also stood out. "She phrases like I phrase. She's a wonderful singer. Everybody knows and loves her very much. I think when they hear this album that we're doing, they're going to say, 'We had no idea that she sings that well.'"

Part of this change in style had to do with the supportive, hospitable recording environment Bennett fostered. "On my earlier records they wanted to make my voice more electronic and Auto-Tuned for radio," Gaga told *Parade*. "That's why this album with Tony is so amazing, because he's hearing me sing raw, without any of that. And he's protecting me from people trying to control what I sound like." On *Cheek to Cheek*, Gaga sounds completely different than she does on her pop records; her croon is rich and luxurious, like crushed velvet, and she has the space to explore greater emotional range.

When the pair convened to record *Cheek to Cheek*, they also went all out instrumentally, hiring dozens of jazz musicians to bring their performances to life. On hand were Bennett's quartet—Mike Renzi, Gray Sargent, Harold Jones, and Marshall Wood—as well as a previous Gaga collaborator, the trumpeter Brian Newman. Dae Bennett, Tony's son, handled the bulk of production—save for on "The Lady Is a Tramp," which also had a credit from the legendary producer Phil Ramone.

Both Gaga and Bennett invoked Amy Winehouse when discussing the album's inspiration. "I thought of her almost every day in the studio," Gaga said during a Twitter Q&A. "I wish she was still here. She was jazz to her core." Added Bennett: "I'm sure that she would be proud and that makes me feel good." Like Winehouse's *Back to Black*, which put an updated spin on retro sounds, the duo's collaborative take on the standards was both fresh and classic. Upbeat songs such as "Goody Goody" and "It Don't Mean a Thing (If It Ain't Got That Swing)" boasted impeccable vocal precision, while her solo take on Cole Porter's "Ev'ry Time We Say Goodbye" is sweetly sad.

Gaga also gravitated toward Billy Strayhorn's "Lush Life," a song she recalled singing as a teenager with the Regis High School boys' choir. "I didn't understand what the lyrics were about, but I understood the melody in a very intense way," she told *Parade*. "Now I know everything that song is about. When I sang it [on this album] for the first time in 15 years, I started crying." Her performance of "Lush Life" on *Cheek to Cheek* is stunning and sophisticated; it's clear she relates especially deeply to the lyrics about loneliness.

Her long-time friends—like her Lower East Side co-conspirator Lady Starlight—were blown away by her turn to jazz. "It just didn't sound like her singing; the quality of the voice, the phrasing, everything, it was so interesting," she told *Rolling Stone*. "For me to hear her sing pop and rock ballads, it made me understand more about her. I could hear how she changed her voice. It was a very cool experience for me." Unsurprisingly, Gaga also switched up her look for the album cycle. Steven Klein, who directed her "Alejandro" video, shot the album cover photograph; Gaga donned a dark-haired wig that bore a striking resemblance to the curly, face-framing hairdo Cher sported in the 1980s.

Cheek to Cheek debuted at number one on the US *Billboard* 200 album charts, selling 131,000 copies during its first week on sale, and also charted well in the UK, Australia,

Above (L-R) *Tony Bennett, Lady Gaga, Cynthia Germanotta, and Joe Germanotta arrive to the Tony Bennett and Lady Gaga* Cheek To Cheek *recording* **Opposite** *Gaga and Bennett perform onstage at The Wiltern on February 8, 2015, in Los Angeles, California*

Right *At the 57th Annual Grammy Awards on February 8, 2015, in Los Angeles, California*

Canada, Greece, Italy, and Japan. It was Gaga's third chart-topping album to date, and helped Bennett set a rather impressive career record: At eighty-eight, he was the oldest artist to land a No. 1 album on the charts. *Cheek to Cheek* also won a Grammy Award for Best Traditional Pop Vocal Album. The concert they taped, *Tony Bennett & Lady Gaga: Cheek to Cheek Live!*, debuted on PBS in October.

Soon after, she and Bennett launched their *Cheek to Cheek* tour, playing festivals (including the Ravinia Festival, the Copenhagen Jazz Festival and the North Sea Jazz Festival) and also performing "Cheek to Cheek" at the Grammy Awards. Their onstage chemistry mirrored what was heard on the album; in fact, they brought out the best in each other.

In February 2015, Gaga took a brief break from her work with Bennett to attend the Oscars and perform a heartfelt tribute to another great songbook: music from 1965's *The Sound of Music*. She was nervous about getting the songs right—so much so that she called the film's star, Julie Andrews, who originated songs like "The Sound of Music," "Do-Re-Mi," "Edelweiss," and "Climb Ev'ry Mountain." "She said, 'I just want to talk to you and make sure I don't offend. That what I'm doing is okay with you,'" Andrews told *People*. "It was very generous of her."

The actress was doubly impressed by Gaga's work ethic. "She said she'd been working so hard and she was singing everything in my keys. I said, 'Why? They're very high, even for me.' And she said, 'Because I wanted to honor you, so I did them in your keys.' That seemed like going one step beyond any place she needed to go." The hard work certainly paid off: Gaga sounded stunning, nailing the songs without breaking a sweat.

She and Bennett reconvened and kept touring through August 2015. And then, a year later, Gaga performed at an event for Bennett's ninetieth birthday party, where she sang "Happy Birthday to You," dueted with Stevie Wonder on "Signed, Sealed, Delivered (I'm Yours)" and unfurled a sultry, jazzy version of "Bad Romance" on solo piano. Other performers might have ended their pairing there; however, Gaga's loyalty and affection for the legend was too strong to

dissipate. "Tony told me Frank Sinatra changed his life when he said 'For my money, Tony Bennett is the best singer in the business,'" Gaga wrote in a Twitter Q&A. "Tony is MY Frank. What he has done for me will change my career forever. And I truly cherish our friendship." Gaga kept her word: She and Bennett recorded a follow-up to *Cheek to Cheek* between 2018 and 2020, a period during which Bennett became increasingly affected by Alzheimer's disease.

In an AARP article revealing the crooner's diagnosis, Gaga is described as an empathetic and tender collaborator who altered her speech patterns specifically to communicate better with Bennett as they spent time together. At another point in the article, she was overcome with emotion after hearing him sing a love song. Her gratitude for his unconditional support—and being able to reciprocate the support he initially gave to her—was even more palpable: "The fact that Tony sees me as a natural-born jazz singer is still something that I haven't gotten over."

Below *Lady Gaga (L) embraces Julie Andrews (R) after performing a* Sound of Music *tribute to the actress, at the 87th Annual Academy Awards*

In July 2021, Gaga and Bennett announced two shows at Radio City Music Hall to celebrate Bennett's ninety-fifth birthday and film a TV special. These shows came with official news of the new album, *Love For Sale*, a collection of Cole Porter covers introduced by a sizzling take on "I Get a Kick Out of You." In a glowing review of the first Radio City Music Hall show, USA *Today* noted the pair dueted together on three of their signature songs: "The Lady Is a Tramp," "Anything Goes," and "It Don't Mean a Thing (If It Ain't Got That Swing)." Bennett was also "as spry and charismatic as ever" during a half-hour solo set that included multiple standing ovations.

Gaga too was in fine form, leaving the stage to sing "La Vie en rose" to her sister Natali ("Sorry, I had to go sing to my sister for a second," she said. "Some things are more important than showbiz") and switching up the lyrics to "New York, New York" to honor her friend and collaborator. "Start spreading the news / it's Tony Bennett's birthday," she sang with her usual brassy verve. "He's my friend. He's my musical companion. He's the greatest singer in the whole world." One might think that Bennett has received more of a boost from working with a younger artist like Gaga. However, it's clear that working with Bennett saved Gaga—and righted the ship of her career.

Above *Lady Gaga sings to Tony Bennett (R) as he celebrates his 90th birthday at The Rainbow Room in New York City, on August 3, 2016*

THE MET GALA

In a 2014 interview with *Harper's Bazaar*, Gaga underscored the deep relationship she has with her flamboyant outfits. "The fashion I've acquired over the years is so sacred to me—from costumes to couture, high fashion to punk wear I've collected from my secret international hot spots. I keep everything in an enormous archive in Hollywood."

Unsurprisingly, Gaga was a regular at the annual Met Gala. For the fashion-obsessed, few events rival the fundraising benefit, which has also been known as the Costume Institute Gala or Met Ball. Attendees are given a different theme to follow each year—and then tasked with putting together outlandish outfits that fit the concept. Gaga was prone to doing exactly this on a regular day, so dressing up for a special event wasn't a stretch.

Gaga made her Met Gala debut in 2010 with a bang, performing "Bad Romance" and "Alejandro" at the event. She didn't walk the red carpet, although she stressed in a later interview she "wasn't nervous," just disinterested. "To be honest with you, I don't give a fuck about red carpets, and I never do them. I don't like them. First of all–how could any of these outfits possibly look good with an ugly red carpet under them?" Gaga herself looked fabulous in two Prada outfits—a plain black suit and a black lace pinafore over a body fishnet stocking—and a head-to-toe Armani sheer bodysuit speckled with crystals.

Her 2015 look for the Met Gala theme "China: Through the Looking Glass" was understated: a Balenciaga creation framed by a kimono-like jacket and cape comprised of cage-netting dotted with feathers. On her head, she wore a simple black headdress; her shoes were chunky platforms. The 2016 Met Gala theme, "Manus x Machina: Fashion in an Age of Technology," felt tailor-made for Gaga. She didn't disappoint, arriving on the red carpet in a Versace jacket that looked like the metallic innards of a computer and a matching silver-and-black striped leotard. Gaga paired that look with impossibly tall metallic spiked boots and tousled blonde hair with dark roots—giving her the look of an eighties sci-fi movie sharpshooter.

And for the 2019 Met Gala, with the theme "Camp: Notes on Fashion," Gaga outdid herself. She walked a fifth of a mile, from 84th and Madison to the steps of the Metropolitan Museum of Art, with an entourage: five dancers, her makeup artist and a photographer. And, for the journey, she wore four outfits conceived by Brandon Maxwell, layered on top of one another.

Gaga's first look was a bright-pink cape dress with a twenty-five-foot train and pillowy sleeves, as well as a matching oversized hair bow; it looked like she crash-landed into a parachute. Next up was a more classic look: a strapless black dress with a corset top and a loose, flowing long skirt. Gaga accessorized the outfit with an umbrella, throwing a whimsical pose that was very golden-age Hollywood. Her third dress was a tube-like hot-pink dress that felt very secret agent-like—a vibe accentuated by rhinestone sunglasses and a Tiffany & Co. choker necklace. Finally, Gaga ended her journey by disrobing into a crystal-studded bra and underwear set with matching, sequined platform boots and fishnets.

Lady Gaga's Met Gala outfits range from simple, like 2015's Balenciaga creation (above), to spectacular, such as the four-outfit ensemble she wore in 2019 (opposite)

9

JOANNE

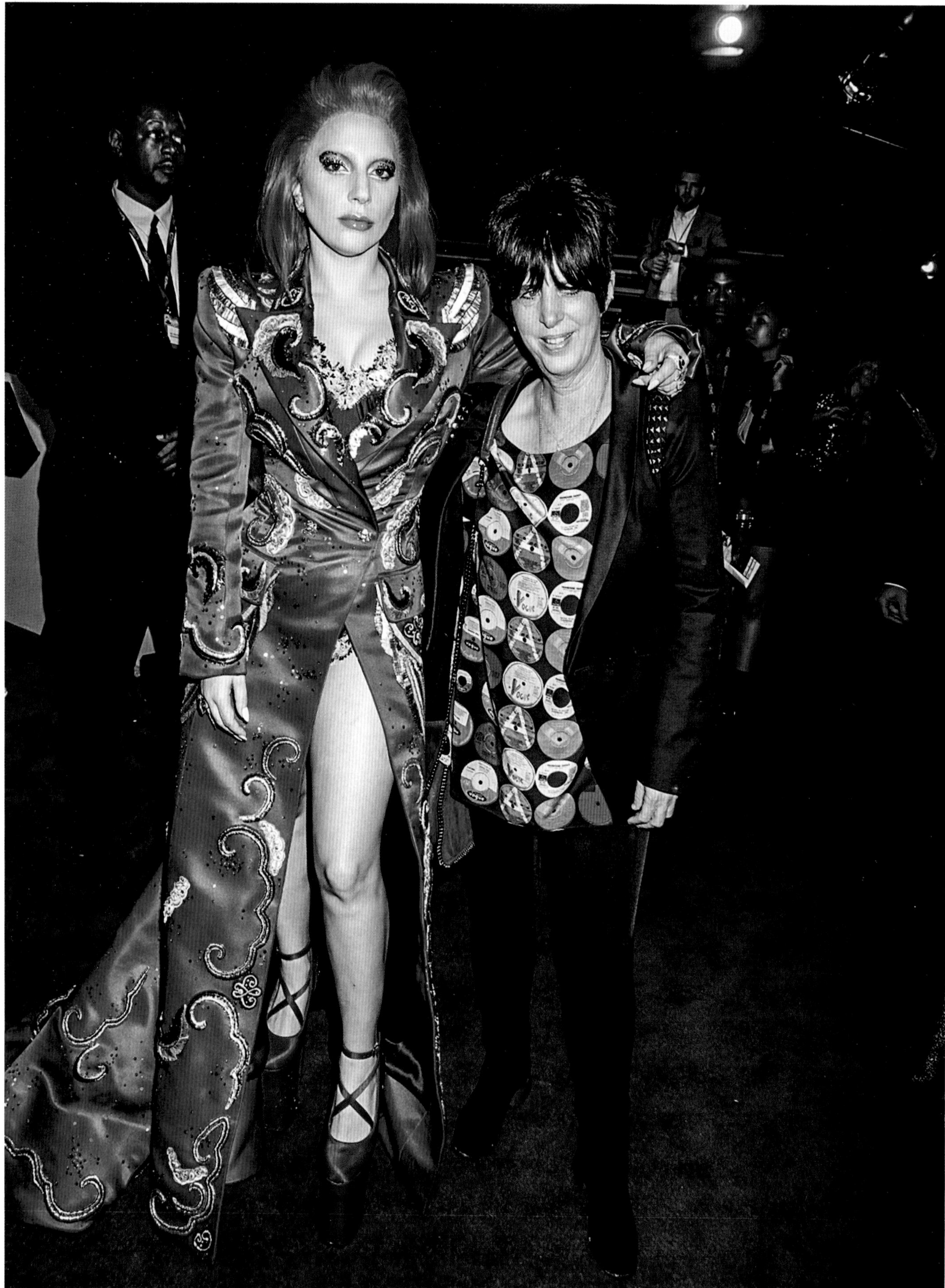

Previous spread *Posing for photographers in front of her new album cover* Joanne *in Tokyo, November 2, 2016*

Opposite *Lady Gaga (L) with songwriter extraordinaire Diane Warren (R) who Gaga teamed up with to pen the song "Til It Happens to You"*

Lady Gaga thrives on collaboration. When Gaga turned her focus back to pop-oriented music after doing *Cheek to Cheek* with Tony Bennett, she teamed up with one of the most successful songwriters in the world: Diane Warren, who's penned hits such as Celine Dion's "Because You Loved Me," Aerosmith's "I Don't Want to Miss a Thing," and LeAnn Rimes's "How Do I Live." In 2015, Gaga and Warren released the stunning "Til It Happens to You," which was heard in *The Hunting Ground*, a documentary about sexual assault on college campuses.

Incredibly enough, the women didn't know each other before collaborating on the song. However, their connection was electric and instantaneous. "We met and I started to play it and sing it and I would say, 'Diane, what do you think of this?'" Gaga recalled during a conversation with Warren on *The Hollywood Reporter*'s *Awards Chatter* podcast. "She took what she already had, and then she gave it to me and she said, 'Make it yours.'" Among other things, Gaga made sure the song didn't come across as downtrodden or defeated, but featured a narrator that wasn't going to let the assault undermine her strength. As Gaga put it: "[The song] became two women together, standing strong."

"Til It Happens to You" certainly had several Warren hallmarks, such as sweeping dynamics and orchestral flourishes. However, Gaga made it her own by adding an understated vocal performance brimming with empathy. The song won a Primetime Emmy Award for Outstanding Original Music and Lyrics, and was nominated for two additional prestigious awards: an Academy Award for Best Original Song and a Grammy Award for Best Song Written for Visual Media. Gaga performed the song at the 2016 Oscars, where she was joined onstage by fifty other survivors of assault. The performance was deeply moving: She wore a simple white suit and played an all-white piano onstage by herself before introducing the survivors—a

"I am so sick of people walking in and out of my life, telling me that I'm gonna be okay because I am still in so much pain that you can't understand."
LADY GAGA

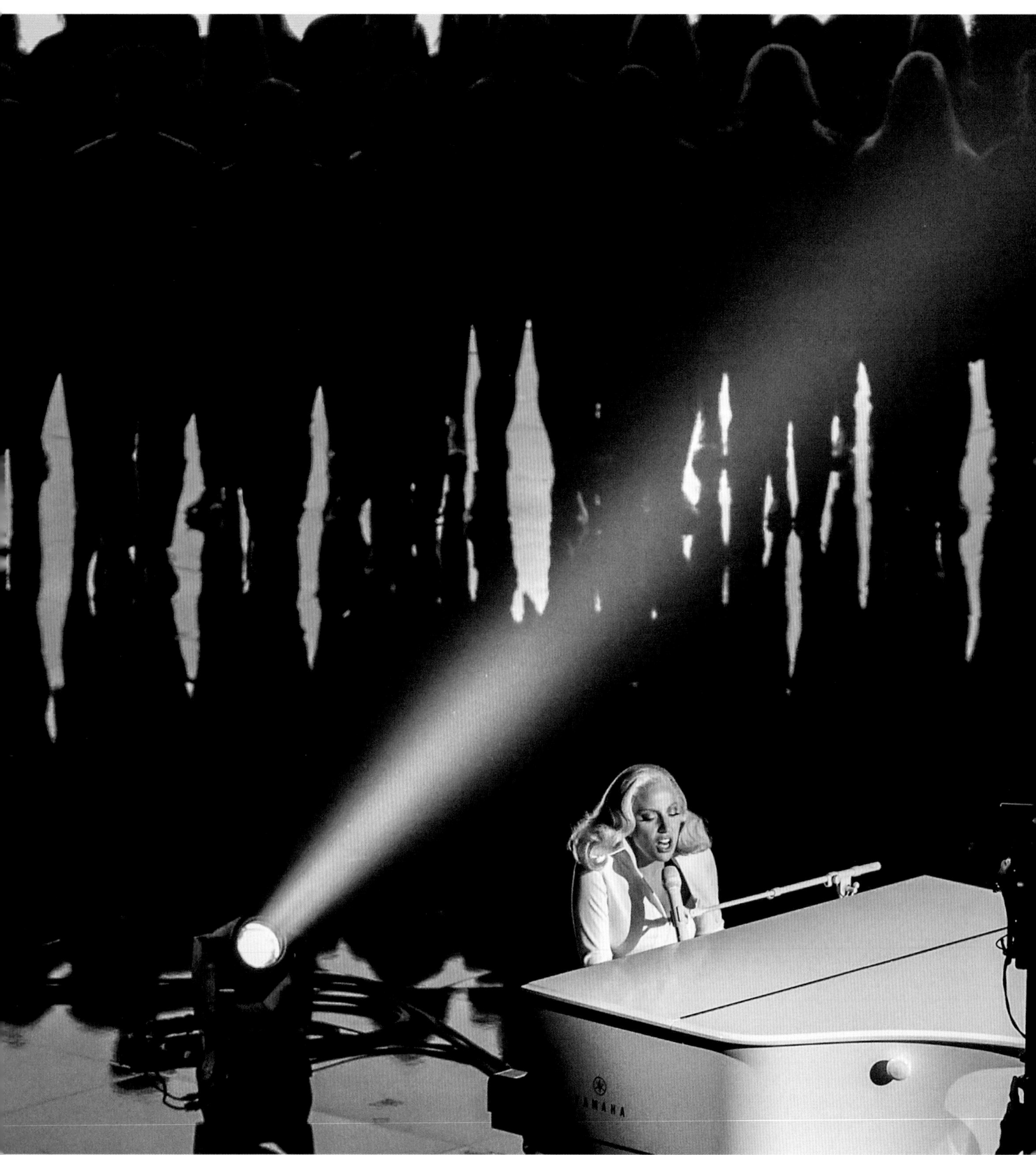

Left *Lady Gaga gives a moving performance of "Til It Happens to You" at the 88th Academy Awards, on February 28, 2016, where she is joined onstage by 50 survivors of sexual assault*

gesture that signified people don't have to go through traumatic experiences by themselves.

In 2015, she also performed the song while receiving Woman of the Year at the Billboard Women In Music Awards. While promoting "Til It Happens to You," Gaga started opening up about her own rape. "I am so sick of people walking in and out of my life, telling me that I'm gonna be okay," Gaga said at one point on *The Hollywood Reporter*'s *Awards Chatter* podcast, "because I am still in so much pain that you can't understand." Gaga later revealed she was assaulted by someone she knew ("It was done to manipulate me in conjunction with money and my music, and it was terrifying") and stressed that the attack still had a profound impact.

"It's something that changed me forever, and it made me question everything about what I had done to be where I am today," she said. "I thought to myself, 'Did I do something wrong to bring this on myself? What did I do?' I choose to wear these clothes, and I choose to dress this way and sing about sex, and you wonder if you're implying to people that it's okay." However, Gaga also noted that the topics brought up in "Til It Happens to You" had deep meaning to her family. "When my father's sister was in college, she was sexually assaulted," Gaga revealed at the 2015 Producers Guild of America Awards. "Then, it tormented her so emotionally that it caused the lupus that she had to get so bad that she died."

Her father's sister, Joanne Germanotta, looms large in Gaga's universe. Joanne's life was tragically short: Born in 1955, she was just nineteen when she died on December 18, 1974. Germanotta is buried in Gate of Heaven Cemetery in East Hanover, New Jersey; an online memorial features a selection of vintage photos of Joanne, as well as virtual flowers and kind notes left by fans.

Her death had a profound impact on her family, Gaga revealed to the *Sunday Times*. "My whole life, I never understood why my father was so sad, drank so much or was wild. I thought it was my fault, and it was painful for the family. I'd witness year after year that feeling of loss within

my father and grandparents. There's something so powerful and deep to lose a child."

Even though Gaga wasn't born when Joanne passed away, her late aunt has always been something of a benevolent guiding presence. Her middle name is Joanne, and she has her aunt's signature and date of death tattooed on her arm, the latter right near text from Rainer Maria Rilke's *Letters to a Young Poet*. In *The Fame*, Gaga published one of Joanne's poems in the album's booklet. And, over the years, she mentioned Joanne consistently in interviews—culminating in a decision to title her fifth studio album, *Joanne*.

In a separate interview, Gaga explained to *People* why now was the right time to honor her father's late sister. "I always wanted to be a good girl," she said. "And Joanne was such a good girl. But I have such a rebellious spirit, and my father was always very angry. He drank because of his sister's death. I was trying to understand him through making this

Above *The Joanne Trattoria restaurant on the Upper West Side, New York, is owned by Gaga's parents, Joe and Cynthia Germanotta, and named after Joe's late sister, Joanne, who died aged nineteen.*

Left *Joe (L) and Cynthia Germanotta (R) with Gaga's grandmother*

record, and in that, also trying to understand why I love men that are cowboys."

The lingering emotion of that time is on display in the 2017 Netflix documentary *Gaga: Five Foot Two*, which covers the making of *Joanne*. In one of the documentary's most affecting moments, Gaga visits her grandmother and reminisces while going through family photographs and old papers, including some of Joanne's writing. "She had a lot of talent but she didn't have enough time," her grandmother said of her beloved daughter, before Gaga plays her the title track via her iPhone. The sadness within the song is palpable even through the tiny speaker; Gaga's father, who's also with them listening, is overcome with emotion and has to leave the room. "That's beautiful," Gaga's grandmother says several times after the song finishes, as the pop star starts crying. "You're just so special." The two then embrace.

Seeing the photos brought Joanne to life, and made it clearer why the woman means so much to Gaga. Speaking to the *New York Times*, Gaga noted that she herself was nineteen—the age Joanne was when she passed—when her musical life began. "I used to leave my apartment and I just had my white boots on and my little shorts and a T-shirt and I would just walk down the street on the Lower East Side totally free. And I had the whole world—the whole unknown of music—and where it could take me ahead of me."

The title track she played for her grandmother is especially meaningful, she added: "And this song ['Joanne'] in a lot of ways I realized even today is me looking back on Joanne and saying 'Where do you think you're going?' You know, I had no idea where I was going." Driven by unadorned acoustic guitar, simple pitter-patter drums and subtle orchestra swells, "Joanne" is indeed a moving farewell to her aunt. At first, the heartfelt song is grief-stricken—Gaga even says that her "aching heart" needs her aunt more than the heavens do—although later on, she is comforted by thoughts of eternal love and the idea that her aunt is thriving in an afterlife as an angel.

Joanne reflected how far Gaga had come since those wild days on the Lower East Side. In fact, two of the album's collaborators, creative directors Ruth Hogben and Andrea

"I always wanted to be a good girl. And Joanne was such a good girl. But I have such a rebellious spirit, and my father was always very angry." LADY GAGA

Gelardin, felt the evolution. The pair had worked with Gaga for close to a decade, but told V magazine that the *Joanne* experience "felt different. Not only is it a change of direction for her as a musician, but also as a woman. *Joanne* is an album by a strong woman, about a strong woman, and this really resonated for us."

Hogben and Gelardin kept this in mind while co-directing the videos for "Perfect Illusion" and "Million Reasons." The former eschewed flamboyant costumes or concepts. Instead, Gaga was in a desert outside Los Angeles, sporting a messy ponytail and plain outfits—a black T-shirt and denim cut-offs, or a grey shirt with sequined hot pants—while dancing around. "We wanted the video to show her without artifice, in a way that her videos may not have done in the past," the pair told V magazine. "There is a simplicity in the concept." They cited the fact she used a handheld mic and drove the car in the video herself as more proof of its directness. "Her commitment to the performance and her authentic raw energy really came across in the way she drove! For us, as directors, it was scary and exciting at the same time—the energy and emotion were purely authentic."

That low-key vibe continued on the video for "Million Reasons," which functioned as a sequel to "Perfect Illusion." Gaga starts off in the same desert, and travels to a gig, where she puts on her *Joanne* wear: the light-pink hat, matching suit and severe eyeliner. The video shifts between black-and-white scenes of her getting ready to perform, and color shots of her singing "Million Reasons," before cresting to its conclusion: She opens a gift box containing a rosary and a note that says, "Love you, sis."

Both songs also felt like sonic departures for Gaga. Tame Impala's Kevin Parker co-wrote and co-produced "Perfect Illusion," ensuring the song's pulsing electro-pop had a lighter touch than previous Gaga dancefloor bangers, while noted country-pop songwriter Hillary Lindsey co-wrote "Million Reasons." Elsewhere, *Joanne* references Motown and country (the harmony-heavy "Come to Mama"), punkish twang ("A-YO") and seventies confessional pop (the warm "Just Another Day").

Speaking to *Entertainment Weekly*, Gaga recalled telling her friend Breedlove she needed a songwriting change around the time *Joanne* came together. "I remember saying, 'You know, I just want to sit at the piano and write songs at the piano and not do anything on a track right now.' He said to me, 'Could you just please fucking make the record that everyone wants you to make?' ... And when your friends that you've known for that long give you that kind of courage as an artist, that's what it's all about, really."

"I used to leave my apartment and I just had my white boots on and my little shorts and a T-shirt and I would just walk down the street on the Lower East Side totally free."

LADY GAGA

Working with producer Mark Ronson also pushed her songwriting into even deeper personal territory, she told the *Associated Press*. "He said to me, 'I know you can write great songs,' [but] he said, '... What do you *have* to write about? That's what I want you to write.'" This advice led to "Grigio Girls," a touching song about her friend Sonja Durham and her journey living with cancer, and "Angel Down," a song inspired by the murder of teenager Trayvon Martin ("Angel down, angel down / But the people just stood around"). "Perfect Illusion," meanwhile, is a breakup song that doubles as a song about the perils of idolatry, while Gaga said "Diamond Heart" is a "completely autobiographical" song about maintaining inner self-confidence (her "diamond heart") despite the odds. "Life is a dog fight for a lot of people," she said in the Genius lyric annotations. "When you find the pitbull within yourself, that's Joanne."

Joanne also featured a bevy of interesting (and even unexpected) guest collaborators. Queens of the Stone Age's Josh Homme added humid guitar scorch to "Diamond Heart," while Gaga duets with Florence Welch of Florence and the Machine on "Hey Girl," a dewy, funky slow jam about the power of friendship. Her collaboration with Beck is an equally funky song, "Dancin' in Circles," that grew out of an impromptu, low-key studio jam. "I think we hung out for two hours, actually, before we even went in," she shared with *Entertainment Weekly*. "We were just talking about life, laying there on the couch, looking out the window."

The Joanne era ushers in a new, low-key look for Lady Gaga as she is sighted out and about in simple ensembles of crop tops and denim hotpants

JUST ANOTHER

Left *Onstage with producer Mark Ronson (R) during Lady Gaga's* Joanne *tour at The Forum, on December 18, 2017, in Inglewood, California*

Some of these names might be surprising to those who only know Gaga's pop side. However, this open-mindedness was a hallmark of *Joanne*. "When I was making *Joanne*, we really had no rules, but that doesn't mean you don't have the intention to see the music with the things that you love," she told *Entertainment Weekly*. "I love a sugary sweet melody. I love a sugary sweet sound that has a message underneath it, or perhaps something darker or different. *Joanne* is not dark in the way that *The Fame Monster* was, but it's dark in a different way. Not darkness as horror—it's dark in the way that things can life be dark."

Joanne debuted at No. 1 on the *Billboard* album charts and was nominated for a Grammy for Best Pop Vocal Album, while "Million Reasons" earned a nod for Best Pop Solo Performance. Perhaps even more important, the album's title track also had a profound impact on Gaga's dad. "I saw a look in my dad's eyes that I've never seen in my whole life," she told the audience during an October 2016 performance at The Satellite in Los Angeles. "Sometimes I used to wonder if I ever got to meet my real dad, you know, because sometimes things happen in your life that are so bad that you die, or a part of you dies." *Joanne*, however, was restorative. "After this record came out, I swear that part of my dad came back to life. I hope that when you hear it when you're with your families and you think of the loss that you've had or the pending loss ... I hope this song can heal you like it healed my family."

Below *Nile Rodgers (L) and Lady Gaga (R) pay tribute to David Bowie at the 58th Grammy Awards in a performance that didn't please everyone*

Fittingly, many elements of the *Joanne* era nodded to her past. At the 2016 Grammy Awards, she teamed up with Nile Rodgers—with whom she had covered Chic's "I Want Your Love" to promote designer Tom Ford's spring/summer collection—and paid tribute to David Bowie. The stirring (and polarizing) medley started with a close-up of her face, as she sings the melancholy "Space Oddity." Through the magic of digital effects, her makeup shifts—blue eyeshadow gives way to an Aladdin Sane lightning bolt—and a spider emerges and crawls around over her nose and eyes. From there, she strutted onto the stage singing "Changes," wearing an appropriately Bowie-esque red close-cropped wig, and busted into a glam medley ("Ziggy Stardust," "Suffragette City," and "Rebel Rebel") and a funkier section where she danced to "Fashion" and "Fame." Rodgers looked gleeful playing the freewheeling riff to "Let's Dance" and added reverence to a triumphant "Heroes."

Reception to the tribute was mixed. Woody Woodmansey, the drummer of The Spiders from Mars—Bowie's backing band named via 1972's concept album, *The Rise and Fall of Ziggy Stardust and the Spiders from Mars*—told NME he and long-time Bowie producer Tony Visconti declined an invitation to take part in the segment after seeing the format. "We looked at it and it was going to be like 14 or 15 songs in the space of four minutes," he said. "And we just went 'No, fuck off, that's stupid, that's not going to represent

Below *Lady Gaga sings the US National Anthem at Super Bowl 50 on February 7, 2016, in Santa Clara, California*

anything good about him.'" Bowie's son Duncan Jones was also less than impressed, tweeting after Gaga's performance, "'Overexcited or irrational, typically as a result of infatuation or excessive enthusiasm; mentally confused.' Damn it! What IS that word!?" Gaga told NME that Jones's reaction "hurt," but added she "did my very best to put together something that I hoped would be the showstopper of the night. All I wanted was for when the Grammys were over, for people to talk of nothing but David Bowie, and I think I achieved that."

That same month, Gaga had a much better response from singing the US national anthem at Super Bowl 50, nailing the high notes with confidence while sporting a metallic red suit. Later in 2016, she did a three-city Dive Bar Tour, which gave her the chance to perform on the roof of her old stomping ground, The Bitter End, as crowds of people swarmed below on the street and cheered her on. And she also did an episode of *Carpool Karaoke* with James Corden, which showed off

Above *Another Super Bowl appearance—headlining the Super Bowl LI Halftime Show, broadcast live from NRG Stadium in Houston, Texas, on February 5, 2017*

how powerful her voice was even without amplification or studio boosts.

On February 5, 2017, she reached another career milestone, as she headlined the Super Bowl LI halftime show at NRG Stadium in Houston, Texas. Ever dramatic, the gig started with her stationed high atop the stadium, singing snippets of "God Bless America" and "This Land Is Your Land," before the scene switched to her taking a huge leap and then descending to the field. Her armor-like, silver-metallic leotard and glittery eye makeup felt like callbacks to *The Fame* era–fitting since she started the show atop an industrial-looking platform singing only a line from "The Edge of Glory" before immediately launching into "Poker Face."

Unlike other Super Bowl halftime shows, Gaga didn't have any high-profile special guests or flashy celebrity cameos. Instead, the entire show focused on her and her formidable catalog of hits. She unleashed "Born This Way" early in the set, where she belted out the song's equality-calling lyrics

Above *Stage diving at the 59th Annual Grammy Awards where Lady Gaga performed with Metallica in a show that didn't go as planned*

in a proud voice, and used a diamond prop for a phone on "Telephone." In another throwback, she threw on a gold spiked jacket and wielded a gigantic keytar to perform "Just Dance" and turned to the piano for "Million Reasons" before ending with a massive take on "Bad Romance." Her performance drew 117.5 million TV viewers in the US alone, making it one of the most-watched Super Bowl halftime shows ever.

In a testament to how unpredictable performing can be, just a few weeks later, what should've been a dynamic Grammy Awards collaboration with Metallica on the band's "Moth Into Flame" went haywire. Gaga was an old-school fan of the metal band—drummer Lars Ulrich later recalled being impressed that she namechecked an early deep cut, "Metal Militia," as a favorite—and practiced her heart out for the performance. "I respect her as an artist," frontman James Hetfield said during an interview on *The Howard Stern Show*. "She was there for two hours before we even got there, working on her moves and thinking stuff up. She is extremely creative and a fearless artist."

Unfortunately, on the awards broadcast, things went awry. Hetfield's mic stopped working, which caused him to have to share a mic with Gaga, and he threw his guitar offstage in frustration. The performance went on, however, albeit chaotically: Gaga shimmied and headbanged all over the stage (including behind Ulrich, who was drumming on a riser that was obscured by flames) and even did a stage dive. However, what the two parties intended didn't quite jell—so much so that Metallica posted their pre-Grammy rehearsal footage, to underscore what the collaboration was meant to sound like.

"I felt embarrassed—I haven't been that angry in a long time," Hetfield told the *New York Post* a few months later. "When something out of my control goes wrong, I still get wound up." However, he added the issues were "a blessing," because he "ended up singing in a microphone with Lady Gaga—maybe even more than she wanted. It felt more like a real collaboration because of that."

In August, Gaga launched the Joanne World Tour. Although there were no shortage of costume changes and elaborate moments—including trippy interstitial videos that depicted (among other things) her having a rhino horn on her forehead and a baggy, bright-red dress for "Bloody Mary"—her outfits and the stage decor were more in line with *Joanne*'s understated vibe. For "A-YO," she strapped on a sparkly guitar and did a little country line dance to the twangy song; "LoveGame" brought a cowboy-sweetheart pale-blue-denim bodysuit with pearl accents and matching boots; and for "Born This Way," she wore a fluffy white tulle skirt and fresh floral-print jacket. However, other parts of the show connected to her past: She hauled around a custom keytar with fringes for "Just Dance," and at other times wielded a gigantic disco stick with a sharp-edged, geometric star on top.

The tour wrapped ten shows early (due to fibromyalgia; in 2017, she had revealed that she lived with the painful condition). Weeks later, she appeared at the March for Our Lives gun-control rally in Washington, D.C. She also did a

Above *Lady Gaga leans on her disco stick at The Forum, California, on August 9, 2017, during her* Joanne World Tour

reverent cover of Elton John's "Your Song" for his tribute album *Revamp: Reimagining the Songs of Elton John & Bernie Taupin* and released a one-off, R&B-inspired single called "The Cure" in April. At the end of the year, *A Star Is Born* hit theaters and changed her life.

In hindsight, being so personal on *Joanne* was "really hard," she told the *Associated Press*. "But it was the best thing I ever did going there, because once you go there, you can't get darker than there 'cause you just got to look inside and whatever it is it is, and then you pick yourself up and keep going." Fearlessness and Gaga have always gone hand-in-hand. But with "Til It Happens to You" and *Joanne*, she made herself vulnerable in new and significant ways.

"The truth is, [*Joanne*] is about being tough," she told *Entertainment Weekly*. "The album is about having endurance and heart no matter how hard things get, and about being unafraid to really look into your heart and how you feel. You have to be willing to listen, and that goes for life and the album. This is an album you really have to listen to. You've got to close your eyes and pay attention."

Above *The Joanne World Tour heats up at Little Caesars Arena on November 7, 2017, in Detroit, Michigan*

HATS

During previous album cycles, Lady Gaga switched up hairstyles and wigs to suit her whims and moods. For example, in 2010, she wore a spiky sun hat that was made using her own hair sprayed into place—and in 2021, before her concerts with Tony Bennett, paparazzi spotted her wearing a very Muppet-like hat comprised of purple feathers.

The cover of *Joanne* was markedly tamer: It featured a very simple photograph of Gaga in profile, sporting a petal-pink cowboy hat made by the L.A.-based milliner Gladys Tamez. Fittingly, the velour hat was from a collection called "Fashion Icons"—and it's named "Marianne," as in the shapeshifting, iconoclastic musician Marianne Faithfull. "Gaga was the first to ever request this hat in pink, because it's her favorite color," Tamez told *The Daily Beast*. "One of the things we talked about were all pastel colors, which are elegant and feminine, so the hats reflect a little bit of the '70s."

According to Tamez, the hat served as something like a muse for Gaga during the *Joanne* era. "She put the hat on and got in the bathtub and started writing the record. It represents more of who she is inside as opposed to her public persona. The hat is central in a symbolic sense to who this new Lady Gaga is." However, the milliner says Gaga is the perfect candidate for headgear: "You need to be super-confident to wear hats, and they play a role in shaping personalities because the first thing a person sees when you walk down the street is your face. When I think of someone, I see their eyes and face and then I envision the hat they'd wear."

Gaga made the most of the pink hat, especially during her October 2016 *Saturday Night Live* appearance, where she added a silvery ribbon for one performance. However, Tamez supplied Gaga with dozens of hats during the *Joanne* era, including a white one and also a version of the "Bianca" (as in Jagger) hat for the subsequent *Joanne* tour. "For Gaga, I tweak the shapes, the colors, and the ribbons," said Tamez. And when Gaga appeared in the Victoria's Secret Fashion Show, the creative outdid herself, crafting a black version of the Joanne hat with 45,700 Swarovski crystals and 60 beaded fringes. According to *Women's Wear Daily* it took ten people and more than three-hundred hours to make—ensuring the hat was a worth a cool million dollars.

"She put the hat on and got in the bathtub and started writing the record. The hat is central in a symbolic sense to who this new Lady Gaga is." GLADYS TAMEZ

A spiky sun hat made using Lady Gaga's own hair (top); The petal-pink cowboy hat worn by Gaga on the cover of her Joanne *album (bottom); and (opposite) a black version of the* Joanne *hat with 45,700 Swarovski crystals and 60 beaded fringes, valued at a cool one million dollars*

10

A FILM STAR IS BORN

Previous spread *Lady Gaga arrives for the premiere of* A Star Is Born *at the 75th Venice Film Festival on August 31, 2018*

Opposite *Singing with Bradley Cooper in* A Star Is Born, *2018*

Celebrities are sometimes reluctant to open up in interviews, which is why *Vogue*'s *73 Questions* video series is so brilliant. Instead of asking questions calibrated to elicit a particular answer, interviewer Joe Sabia fires off open-ended queries that often bring about illuminating and even philosophical responses.

When Sabia visited Lady Gaga before a 2018 *Vogue* cover story, her nonchalant demeanor nevertheless couldn't hide the heart on her sleeve. "What's something you're proud to say is now behind you?" he asked early on in the gentle interrogation, and she responded right away, "You know, all the negative stuff that happens in your twenties."

Her savvy response had more than a kernel of truth. In the accompanying print feature, she ruminated on the previous decade, which found her rising from New York City dive-bar denizen to glam global superstar and then leading lady in a new version of *A Star Is Born*. "There has been a galaxy of change," she said. "I would just say that it's been a nonstop whirlwind. And when I am in an imaginative or creative mode, it sort of grabs me like a sleigh with a thousand horses and pulls me away and I just don't stop working."

In a thoughtful tone, she spelled out the good—and the bad—of this change. "You ... make friends, you lose friends, you build tighter bonds with people you've known for your whole life. But there's a lot of emotional pain, and you can't really understand what it all means until ten years has gone by."

Part of this sadness emerged in *Gaga: Five Foot Two*, in which she talked about losing the loves of her life as she became more successful and her career took off; most recently, she and Taylor Kinney cancelled their engagement in 2016, after she signed up for *A Star Is Born*. "I did a movie and lose Taylor," she said. "This is the third time I've had my heart broken like this."

"She had her hair slicked back, and she sang 'La Vie en rose,' and I was just ... levitating."
BRADLEY COOPER

Gaga also continued to deal with multiple physical health problems, most notably fibromyalgia, a disorder marked by chronic pain in places such as muscles and joints. *Gaga: Five Foot Two* shows her on a couch in anguish, and also at the doctor seeking relief. "I get so irritated with people who don't believe fibromyalgia is real," she told *Vogue*. "For me, and I think for many others, it's really a cyclone of anxiety, depression, PTSD, trauma, and panic disorder, all of which sends the nervous system into overdrive, and then you have nerve pain as a result. People need to be more compassionate. Chronic pain is no joke. And it's every day waking up not knowing how you're going to feel."

Opposite *Lady Gaga as The Countess Elizabeth in* American Horror Story: Hotel **Above** *Lady Gaga as La Chameleón in* Machete Kills

Despite the discord hinted at in *Gaga: Five Foot Two* and the *Vogue* story, Gaga was on the verge of fulfilling one childhood dream: becoming a big-time actress, starring opposite Bradley Cooper in his directorial debut, a modern take on *A Star Is Born*. Gaga called her version of the film a "traveling legacy," not a re-do, which is key.

French movie posters for Machete Kills, *2013 (above) and* Sin City: A Dame to Kill For, *2014 (opposite, top); both directed by Robert Rodriguez*

Oppposite, bottom *Lady Gaga as witch Scáthach in* American Horror Story: Roanoke

The movie originated as a 1937 Technicolor film starring Janet Gaynor and Fredric March, with a premise based around a hopeful young actress, not musician. The 1954 musical version was a critical success: Co-stars Judy Garland and James Mason both won Golden Globe Awards for their roles, and the soundtrack became a beloved favorite. *A Star Is Born*'s profile soared even higher in 1976 with the Kris Kristofferson-Barbra Streisand version, which won the Academy Award for Best Original Song at 1977's Oscars for the theme, "Evergreen."

Over the years, many musicians had been considered for the main role of a new *A Star Is Born*, including Jennifer Lopez and Beyoncé. However, Cooper officially signed on for the re-make in 2016, and decided to hire Gaga as his co-star after catching her performing at a backyard cancer benefit.

"She had her hair slicked back, and she sang 'La Vie en rose,' and I was just ... levitating," he recalled to *Vogue*. "It shot like a diamond through my brain. I loved the way she moved, the sound of her voice." The very next day, he drove to Malibu—and Gaga had a similar jolt of recognition and familiarity. "The second that I saw him, I was like, 'Have I known you my whole life?'" she told *Vogue*. "It was an instant connection, instant understanding of one another.'"

Over a lunch of spaghetti and meatballs, the pair started talking and then ended up performing the traditional folk song "Midnight Special." Gaga, who was on piano, was blown away by Cooper's voice. "He sings from his gut, from the nectar!" she told *Vogue*. "I knew instantly: This guy could play a rock star. And I don't think there are a lot of people in Hollywood who can. That was the moment I knew this film could be something truly special." Gaga had the foresight to film their duet on her phone; Cooper showed the video to Warner Bros., which helped the movie move forward into production.

By the time *A Star Is Born* started filming, Gaga had plenty of professional acting experience and voiceover work under her belt. There were her holiday variety shows, of course, but also a 2012 voiceover appearance on *The Simpsons*, where she was tasked with elevating the mood of Lisa Simpson and the rest of Springfield. She also appeared in two Robert Rodriguez films, 2013's *Machete Kills* and 2014's *Sin City: A Dame to Kill For*.

In late 2015, she started portraying her biggest role yet: the murder-loving Countess in *American Horror Story: Hotel*. Gaga called playing this role "a dream come true," in no small part due to the show's creator Ryan Murphy, whom she said believed in her when others didn't. "With Ryan, soulmate feels like too small of a word because it implies it's someone

with whom you will spend the rest of your life," she said in an interview published on the website of her childhood acting school. "But I know that with Ryan, through this role, he gave me a sense of self beyond what I believed I was."

Gaga approached The Countess role with her usual intensity, drawing on her years studying method acting to become fully absorbed in her character, who favored luxe fashions. "I become The Countess in the car on my way to work," she continued. "I put fishnet on my face and red lipstick on and I read my lines. I am always prepared before I come to the trailer." Her dedication to the craft paid off: On January 10, 2016, she won a Golden Globe for Best Performance by an Actress in a TV Movie or Miniseries for the role.

Quipping that she felt like Cher in the 1987 film *Moonstruck*, she accepted the award by calling it "one of the greatest moments of my life." After thanking Murphy and her cast mates, she declared, "Because of you, I was able to shine, I guess. So thank you for sharing your talent with me. I wanted to be an actress before I wanted to be a singer, but music worked out first." She followed up the award-winning part by returning to the series in fall 2016, where she portrayed a witch named Scáthach, in *American Horror Story: Roanoke*. In contrast to The Countess, Scáthach was grittier and scarier, with a matted, red-brown wig and dirty makeup.

A Star Is Born started production in April 2017 at Coachella, specifically during the week of downtime between both weekends of the festival. (Gaga happened to be headlining the real thing.) "We had the run of the entire place, all the stages, for five days," Cooper told *Entertainment Weekly*. "It was the first stuff we shot. That was amazing because that was the first time I sang on stage with her. I couldn't believe how easy it was."

For authenticity, they continued to film at actual music festival sites, including the country-leaning Stagecoach—a scene shot in eight minutes "between Jamey Johnson and Willie Nelson," Cooper recalled—and in front of a packed crowd of eighty-thousand people at Glastonbury in England. The latter was something of a full-circle moment: Kris Kristofferson, co-star of the award-winning 1976 musical version of *A Star Is Born* himself, let Cooper share the stage. "[He] was kind enough to give us four minutes of his set," the actor revealed. "I sang, played the guitar solo, and then I said, 'Ladies and gentlemen, Kris Kristofferson.'"

Gaga found some other parallels to her career in the script, such as when Cooper (as Jackson Maine) finishes a performance and comes offstage to dead silence. "This

Right *Filming for* A Star Is Born *at actual music festival sites; in front of eighty-thousand people at Glastonbury in the UK*

is how I feel as a performer," she explained to *Elle*. "That's what it feels like when you go onstage and there are 20,000 people screaming ... and then the show is over and there's no sound. It's emotional." But while it might be easy to say she and Ally were one and the same, that's far from the case. "The character of Ally is informed by my life experience," Gaga continued. "But I also wanted to make sure that she was not me. It was a cadence of both."

For proof of that, she revealed to *Elle* that there were *some* growing pains throughout filming, including at the first scene she and Cooper did together in a Mexican restaurant. "Bradley got some tacos and brought them to the table," she recalled. "Then he said something to me, but it wasn't what was in the script, and I didn't know what to do, so I just said my line. Then he said something else, and I didn't know what to do because I thought I was just supposed to be saying what was on the page." Flustered, she just said what was next

Above (L-R) *Anthony Rossomando, Andrew Wyatt, Lady Gaga, and Mark Ronson pose with their award for Best Original Song for "Shallow" at the 76th Annual Golden Globe Awards*

in the script, to which Cooper responded asking if she was okay. "I just started to cry," she said.

This inexperience ultimately helped her interactions with Cooper, as Ally's awe at being wooed by a famous musician felt natural and realistic. And while Gaga clearly drew on her upbringing and early days in music for *A Star Is Born*, it was no biopic. Although many musicians are self-conscious when they switch to movies—or end up portraying thinly veiled versions of their real selves—Gaga disappeared fully into the role of Ally, an aspiring singer who's thrust into the spotlight after a chance encounter with troubled rock star Jackson Maine. Early on, when she wows the crowd at a drag bar by singing "La Vie en rose," she dials back any Gaga-isms and channels her more theatrical side. Later, when her character becomes a pop star named Ally (no last name) her approach to pop is more muted and conventional than Gaga's take—and she pulls it off.

Above *Lady Gaga dazzles the audience at the 61st Annual Grammy Awards, where she also picked up two more awards for "Shallow"*

Right *Bradley Cooper and Lady Gaga give a heart-stirring performance of "Shallow" at the 91st Annual Academy Awards on February 24, 2019, in Hollywood, California*

In light of this, Gaga's acting drew raves. "Pop singer Lady Gaga is quite good as the wife," wrote the *Chicago Reader*. "She subtly and convincingly manages the character's transformation from vulnerable ingenue to self-confident celebrity." *The Observer* (UK) stated the movie was "as deep and resonant as Bradley Cooper's drawl, and as bright as Lady Gaga's screen future," while *The Spectator* said Gaga was "truly sensational, fabulous, a revelation. I had no idea." *The Boston Globe*, meanwhile, observed, "The role of Ally is so meta as to cast doubt on whether Lady Gaga can play other kinds of parts; the performance is so galvanizing that you don't remotely care."

Gaga did admit a deep kinship to her character. "I feel Ally inside of me," she told *Variety* in fall 2018. "I wonder how long she'll stay. Or if she'll be in there forever." In fact, she snuck in to see the movie during its theatrical run, but had to leave before the film ended because she was so overcome with emotion. "I had to remove myself before the end," she told *Variety*. "The film moves me so deeply. I feel so entrenched in the character that the second half of the film—without revealing what happens—is so emotional and tragic. I have to take myself out of it."

A Star Is Born premiered at the Venice Film Festival in August 2018 but opened in US theaters on October 5. The movie earned $42.9 million in the US during its opening weekend, good enough for second at the box office behind *Venom*. Overall, the movie made $215.3 million in the US and Canada. In addition to box office success, the film also had a hit soundtrack that topped the charts around the world, including in the US, UK, and Canada. Produced in part by country whiz Dave Cobb, the *A Star Is Born* soundtrack featured a mix of covers and original songwriting contributions from Gaga and some of Nashville's finest songwriters: Jason Isbell, Natalie Hemby, Hillary Lindsey, Lori McKenna, and Lukas Nelson. Appropriately, the album is full of rugged Americana and country rock, spliced with doses of seventies classic rock and folk.

Together, Gaga and Cooper also had a major crossover pop smash with the searing duet "Shallow." Co-written by

Gaga, Mark Ronson, Anthony Rossomando, and Andrew Wyatt, the song (rightfully) dominated the 2019 awards show season. A conversation between two people who aren't quite connecting, "Shallow" is about being over your head in a relationship, teetering on the edge of drowning but trying to find a solution to make things work. Near the middle of the song, Gaga goes to her higher range and bellows, "I'm off the deep end, watch as I dive in / I'll never meet the ground," which propels the song to soaring emotional heights. The anguish she feels because of her partner seared like a brand.

A *Star Is Born* itself also received dozens of award nominations, including multiple individual acting nods for Gaga and Cooper. At the Golden Globe Awards in early January, Gaga lost the Best Performance in a Motion Picture – Drama award to Glenn Close, but won Best Original Song for "Shallow." She looked fantastic nonetheless, sporting a strapless, baby-blue Valentino couture dress with billowing sleeves, and a simple topknot dyed the same color as the frock. A few weeks later, when the Oscar nominations were announced, any disappointment dissipated: She was nominated for the coveted Best Actress and Best Original Song awards. Incredibly enough, she was only the second person ever to receive nominations for both acting and songwriting for the same film in a given year; only Mary J. Blige had achieved this feat previously, for 2017's *Mudbound*.

Cooper and Gaga blurred fantasy and reality for their performance of "Shallow" at the Oscars. As a guitarist played the song's heart-stirring acoustic riff offscreen, the couple walked up to the stage from the front row, hand-in-hand. Cooper sang the first verse directly to Gaga, who stood still before sitting down at the piano and taking the lead. Her voice grew in passion and intensity until the song's electric ending, which culminated with Cooper joining her on the piano bench to end the performance singing together at one mic. The intimate duet captured the delicacy and turbulence of their characters' onscreen relationship.

Unsurprisingly, "Shallow" took home the Academy Award for Best Original Song. A tearful Gaga, wearing a halter-neckline black Brandon Maxwell dress, thanked her family and co-writers, before saving perhaps her biggest compliment for Cooper: "Thank you for believing in us." She again lost the acting award, this time to Olivia Colman, but picked up two more awards for "Shallow" at the Grammys that February. Her performance of the song there hewed toward devilish glam: She fronted a sleek electric rock band while sporting a jewel-bedecked catsuit and Bowie-caliber high boots. When all was said and done, Gaga became the first woman ever to win an Oscar, Grammy, Golden Globe, and a BAFTA in the same year. For good measure, during the week of March 9, "Shallow" hit No. 1 on the *Billboard* Hot 100 singles chart.

"I feel Ally inside of me. I wonder how long she'll stay. Or if she'll be in there forever."

LADY GAGA

Despite any losses, Gaga's acting career—and the *A Star Is Born* soundtrack—had incredible momentum. After having success in 2019, the album also won two Grammys in 2020, for Best Compilation Soundtrack for Visual Media and Best Song Written for Visual Media for "I'll Never Love Again." In late 2019, Gaga was cast as the lead in Ridley Scott's long-gestating biopic on the Gucci family. Gaga was to portray Patrizia Reggiani, or Lady Gucci, who has a sordid past: *Variety* notes she "was tried and convicted of orchestrating" the assassination of her ex-husband, family patriarch Maurizio Gucci. Couture luxe fashion and dramatic Italian family stories—Gaga seemed tailor made for the role.

Opposite *Lady Gaga poses with her Oscar for Best Original Song. In 2019, she became the first woman ever to win an Oscar, Grammy, Golden Globe, and a BAFTA in the same year.*

CHROMATICA

Previous spread AT&T TV *Super Saturday Night with Lady Gaga, February 1, 2020, Miami, Florida*

Opposite *Lady Gaga onstage during her Vegas residency, in December, 2018*

Years ago, Las Vegas residencies were reserved for veteran artists considered washed-up or in the twilight of their careers. Playing Vegas was a last resort or final career stop, not a badge of honor. However, thanks to the blockbuster residences booked by acts such as Celine Dion and Britney Spears, as well as the proliferation of mega-dance clubs anchored by superstar DJs, current-day Vegas is a cool, in-demand musical locale.

In late December 2018, Lady Gaga made a splash in Vegas with a high-profile residency. The concert skillfully nodded to Sin City's split personality: One version of the show was an over-the-top pop extravaganza called Enigma, while another one was a classy, old-fashioned revue dubbed Jazz & Piano. Gaga's the rare modern pop star who can pull off both musical styles equally well, meaning either concert was a satisfying watch.

According to a *Rolling Stone* review, the pop show was narrated by an "alien guardian angel" who warned that Gaga can only move forward in life if she revisits and embraces the past. (Call it a cutting-edge, modern version of A *Christmas Carol*.) She set a futuristic vibe from song one, sailing over the crowd while wearing a crystal-encrusted bodysuit, and then performing "Just Dance" while suspended in the air, clutching a keytar. From there, the career-spanning set touched on all eras and vibes—she and dancers sported neon-hued costumes and rave wear for "Beautiful, Dirty, Rich," "Aura" and "Applause"—and unleashed some jaw-dropping stage props. For "Scheiße," Gaga wore steely armor and stood in the midst of a gigantic, multi-arm robot waving its appendages, while her piano had gigantic splinters as if it was a fraying rock formation. She also redeemed her 2016 Grammys performance with a brief, industrial-thrashed snippet of David Bowie's "I'm Afraid of Americans" at the end of one section.

"I live on Chromatica, that is where I live. I went into my frame. I found Earth, I deleted it. Earth is cancelled. I live on Chromatica."
LADY GAGA

Jazz & Piano, meanwhile, highlighted her more grown-up, straitlaced *Cheek to Cheek*. Bennett even performed "Cheek to Cheek" and "The Lady Is a Tramp" with her at a January 2019 show. The crowd screamed and cheered on his appearance like he was a rock god. "Is he something or what?" Gaga said, and quipped, "He walks into the room, everybody stands up. I gotta hold a note for 30 seconds." Enigma was a roaring success, grossing $53.87 million in 2019 and pushing Gaga over the $500 million mark for career touring earnings, making her only the fifth woman to achieve this milestone. The residency was due to restart in spring 2020, until the COVID-19 pandemic forced the show to go dark until further notice.

Still, as usual, Gaga had plenty going on. In 2019, she launched a vegan and cruelty-free makeup line called Haus Laboratories. And, in 2020, she revealed something else brewing: *Chromatica*, her sixth studio album and first straight-up pop effort since 2013's ARTPOP. If the album

Above *Lady Gaga showcases Enigma—a pop extravaganza—at Park Theater, Park MGM, on December 28, 2018*

title also sounds kind of like the name of a glittery distant planet, you'd be correct. "I live on Chromatica, that is where I live," she said in a radio interview promoting the LP. "I went into my frame. I found Earth, I deleted it. Earth is cancelled. I live on Chromatica." The planet, naturally, was welcoming to all.

To beam listeners to *Chromatica*, she teamed up with some familiar names (producer BloodPop and musicican Madeon, her old pal Justin Tranter, Elton John, Max Martin) and a bevy of cutting-edge electro collaborators, including SOPHIE, Swedish House Mafia's Axwell, Boys Noize, Morgan Kibby, and Skrillex. "It felt right for her to revisit electronic elements, so we came straight out of the gates with pulsating synths and house rhythms," BloodPop told *Entertainment Weekly*, noting that the "Enigma" demo kickstarted the album's direction. "It was more about her vocal performance than anything, and how she wrapped around that track. It felt powerful.... It felt like a mix of

Above *Gaga sets a futuristic vibe, suspended above the crowd in a crystal-encrusted bodysuit while playing a keytar*

Studio 54 and threads of all our favorite dance records. It evoked that fleeting, euphoric feeling that comes from good dance music."

Indeed, *Chromatica* has a distinctly throwback vibe that touches on glittery seventies disco, kicky eighties new wave and triumphant nineties house music. "We weren't going for modern EDM, we were going for classic-feeling dance music," producer BURNS told *Entertainment Weekly*. "'Authentic' was a word I used a lot; it had to be familiar, but also fresh at the same time." To that end, "Alice" boasts a Korg M1 organ bass, while BURNS added, "I was conscious of trying to steer away from that polished, crisp sound you hear in a lot of current pop-EDM production. I wanted everything I was a part of to have character and a bit of grit to it."

That same vibe extended to the album's videos. "Rain on Me" featured Ariana Grande, Gaga and a bevy of dancers celebrating in a dark (and, yes, damp) post-apocalyptic scene, while looking like cutting-edge club kids. Fittingly, designer Laura Pulice told *Entertainment Tonight* she created "a futuristic sci-fi punk" magenta-pink latex bodysuit for Gaga, molding her into "a heavy metal album sex symbol." For Grande, she made a sleeveless latex bodysuit and matching skirt in pale purple, noting, "We wanted to keep with the style that she's comfortable with, while staying with the futuristic theme of the video."

Below and opposite *The flip side of her Vegas residency: Lady Gaga Jazz & Piano*

"Stupid Love," meanwhile, was the lighter side of the end-of-the-world dance club. The song came with an iPhone-shot video *Paper* described as a "dystopian Pride tea dance, with warring *Mad Max*-like tribes who are more likely to be fighting over Haus Beauty samples than drinking water." Seemingly set on Planet Chromatica, Gaga leads a gang of pink-clad revelers while wearing a risqué outfit: satin bra, underwear studded with spikes, a high ponytail and long hair extensions, and a heart-shaped forehead charm. In a nod to the song's positive vibe, the crews dance around—and, at one point, Gaga uses telekinesis to separate two dancers who start sparring. The message is clear: Choose love and unity, not violence.

The uplift was at odds with the album's rollout: *Chromatica*'s release was initially delayed due to the COVID-19 pandemic, which began to surge just as promotion started. In an interview, Gaga also opened up to Oprah Winfrey about the sexual assault she had first started talking about in 2014. Much had changed in the past six years: The #MeToo movement rippling through the entertainment industry inspired celebrities in multiple industries to come forward about their experiences, while conversations about mental health were more common and encouraged. Gaga was more honest than she had ever been, revealing she became pregnant from the assault and had a "total psychotic break" afterward that brought on a diagnosis of PTSD. "For a couple years, I was not the same girl."

This wasn't the only trauma she revisited. In an Apple Music interview, she confessed to host Zane Lowe that

HAUS
LABORATORIES

she thought she fell short with an aim of *Joanne*: easing the pain her dad felt from his sister's death. This particular admission contradicted what she had said in the wake of *Joanne*'s release—that her dad had felt some relief—which made her statement much sadder.

Writing and recording *Chromatica* itself also brought up some difficult emotions that weighed heavily on her. "I used to wake up in the morning, and I would realize I was 'Lady Gaga.' And then I became very depressed and sad, and I didn't want to be myself," she told *People*. "I felt threatened by the things my career brought into my life and the pace of my life." This heavy mood affected her creativity, she added: "I spent a lot of time in a sort of catatonic state of just not wanting to do anything. And then I finally, slowly started to make music and tell my story through my record."

Understandably, *Chromatica* boasts some of the most vulnerable lyrics of her career. The first non-instrumental

Opposite *Lady Gaga celebrates the launch of her own makeup line, Haus Laboratories in 2019* **Above** *Ariana Grande (L) and Lady Gaga (R) perform during the 2020 MTV Video Music Awards*

song "Alice" (as in Wonderland) captured the uncertainty she felt. "It's this weird experience where I'm going, 'I'm not sure I'm going to make it, but I'm going to try,'" she said in the Genius lyric annotations. "And that's where the album really begins." "Replay" is about the claustrophobic and painful experience of being forced to re-live past traumas: "The scars on my mind are on replay, r-replay / The monster inside you is torturing me." However, the sentiment of "Rain on Me" is that she'd rather be open about her life, warts and all, than keep it hidden: "Gotta live my truth, not keep it bottled in / So I don't lose my mind, baby."

One of *Chromatica*'s other highlights, "911," references an antipsychotic medication called Olanzapine, which she takes "because I can't always control things that my brain does," she told Apple Music. Appropriately, the song's surreal, brightly colored video reflects the spatial and mental disorientation that might occur without this pharmaceutical help. Gaga worked with filmmaker Tarsem

Above *Gaga opens up to Oprah on Oprah's 2020 Vision: Your Life in Focus Tour, January 4, 2020, in Sunrise, Florida*

Singh, who won an MTV Video Music Award for R.E.M.'s "Losing My Religion" in 1991 but hadn't directed a music video in twenty-two years. The "911" short film is like many Gaga clips, as it references imagery found in movies—in this case, a 1969 Armenian movie called *The Colour of Pomegranates*. The camera perspectives tip and rotate, as Gaga—who sports turquoise-streaked hair and matching eye shadow—experiences scenes that include a man throwing his head repeatedly onto a pillow and a woman cradling a plaster figure.

As it turns out, the scenes took place in her head after a car accident. Gaga is strapped to a backboard while EMTs attend to her health and soothe her as she wails about her lack of pills. On Instagram, she wrote that the video covers "the way reality and dreams can interconnect to form heroes within us and all around us," and thanked her fans for their support. "Thank you for believing in me when I was very afraid. Something that was once my real life everyday is now a film, a true story that is now the past and not the present. It's the poetry of pain."

"I've been open about the fact that I have had masochistic tendencies that are not healthy. They're ways of expressing shame. They're ways of expressing feeling not good enough, but actually they're not effective. They just make you feel worse."
LADY GAGA

The realization that she can move forward from trauma turned out to be one of *Chromatica*'s most poignant themes. "Free Woman" especially was her way of reclaiming her truth due to her assault, with lyrics such as "This is my dancefloor I fought for / A heart, that's what I'm livin' for." In the lyrical annotations on Genius, she added, "I tend to aspire for things to be genderless. [It was] significant to reference my gender because I was assaulted by a music producer. I no longer am going to define myself as a survivor or as a victim."

That strength resonated with fans, as *Chromatica* debuted at No. 1 in the US and UK, and also topped the charts in Austria, Italy, New Zealand, Portugal, and Switzerland, among other countries. "I think that the beginning of the album really symbolizes, for me, what I would call the beginning of my journey to healing, and what I would hope would be an inspiration for people that are in need of healing through happiness, through dance," Gaga told Apple Music, saying she terms this as "radical acceptance" in her own life. "For example, I know that I have mental issues; I know that they can be sometimes rendering me nonfunctional as a human. But I radically accept that this is real."

Perhaps even more important, Gaga added that she forgave herself "for all the ways I've punished myself in private," such as cutting herself. "I've been open about the fact that I have had masochistic tendencies that are not healthy. They're ways of expressing shame. They're ways

Above *Limited-edition, Gaga-themed Oreos available to buy with the release of* Chromatica

Right *At the 2020 MTV Muisc Video Awards accepting the Best Collaboration award for "Rain on Me," written with Ariana Grande*

of expressing feeling not good enough, but actually they're not effective. They just make you feel worse."

However, not everything about the *Chromatica* era was painful. For example, fans could buy limited-edition Gaga-themed Oreos of pale-pink cookies and sea foam-green filling. And, despite challenges related to social distancing and the pandemic lockdown, Gaga brought nine different looks to the 2020 MTV Video Music Awards. Her red carpet fashion choice was astronaut chic: She paired a clear bubble helmet and black platform boots with a flowing dress made out of silver material, making her appear swaddled in aluminum foil. Later, she donned a series of elaborate face masks—including a robotic one that featured red and white sine waves in time with her singing voice—and performed "911" and "Rain on Me," the latter with Grande as special guest.

For good measure, she also won five awards, including for Artist of the Year, Song of the Year, Best Cinematography, Best Collaboration for "Rain on Me," and the first-ever Tricon Award, given to artists talented in multiple creative disciplines. "Rain on Me" also won a Best Pop Duo/Group Performance Grammy—the first time, incredibly enough, a duet with two women won this category—and became yet another global blockbuster chart success, hitting No. 1 in the US and countless other places.

Due to the COVID-19 pandemic, her proposed Chromatica Ball tour had to be bumped to late 2020. Ever restless, however, Gaga curated 2020's One World: Together at Home, a benefit concert put together in tandem with the World Health Organization. The event featured performances by The Rolling Stones, Billie Eilish, Paul McCartney, Tom Jones and others, as well as greetings from Matthew McConaughey, Lupita Nyong'o, Michelle Obama, and Oprah Winfrey. All told, One World: Together at Home earned an amazing $127 million for COVID-19 relief efforts.

Gaga worked on the fundraiser with multiple people, including her boyfriend, a Harvard graduate and tech entrepreneur named Michael Polansky. The cute couple

first went public in early February 2020 via an adorable Instagram photo featuring Gaga curled up in Polansky's lap, as he looks at her with an adoring gaze. They were spotted together on social media after that, including when *Chromatica* was released: On Instagram, Gaga posted a video of them dancing to the song "911" along with helium-filled balloons that spelled out "Chromatica."

During one of the most fraught times in modern history, the optimistic outlook of *Chromatica* ended up inspiring not just Gaga, but the world. "On my new album, I want everyone to know that even if life is painful sometimes, you can still dance through it," she told *Vogue*. "You can dance through it because you're being brave by fighting the pain and living life. This is something that should be celebrated. This is a reason to dance."

Above *With new beau, Michael Polansky on February 2, 2020*

12

RE-BORN THIS WAY

Previous spread *Lady Gaga leaves the Plaza Hotel in New York City, on July 2, 2021*

Opposite *Lady Gaga enjoys a close relationship with mom, Cynthia (L)*

"I'm just really grateful that my mom holds space for me to be able to talk about how I feel. And because of that, we have a very healthy relationship that is beautiful." LADY GAGA

Although the pandemic prevented Lady Gaga from touring in 2020 and into 2021, she was never far from the spotlight. Multiple songs on *Chromatica* were released as remixes, while she became the face of the new Valentino perfume Voce Viva in fall 2020. Gaga and her mom, Cynthia, also co-wrote a book, *Channel Kindness: Stories of Kindness and Community*, that featured more than fifty inspiring stories from young people, and spawned a website that gives people a chance to share more moments of kindness. Speaking to *People*, Gaga brought up her rough middle school years, when she was bullied and felt depressed, and how difficult it was to share these feelings. "When I was younger and had mental issues, my mom didn't know how to communicate with me about it. We've found a way to channel kindness into our lives in a way that's also healed our relationship."

Her mom, Cynthia, added that she didn't grow up knowing how to be open and vulnerable about emotions, and expressed gratitude that she can now be "open and honest" with her famous daughter. "I'm just really grateful that my mom holds space for me to be able to talk about how I feel," Gaga added. "And because of that, we have a very healthy relationship that is beautiful."

In early 2021, Gaga had the honor of singing the National Anthem at the inauguration of the forty-sixth president of the United States, Joe Biden. The day before, she posted a photo of herself in Washington, D.C. wearing a sleek Givenchy white cape dress, alongside a heartfelt wish for tranquility. "I pray tomorrow will be a day of peace for all Americans," she wrote. "A day for love, not hatred. A day for acceptance not fear. A day for dreaming of our future joy as a country. A dream that is non-violent, a dream that provides safety for our souls."

On the actual Inauguration Day, she performed while wearing a subtly patriotic custom outfit designed by Daniel Roseberry: a form-fitting navy cashmere jacket with a gigantic

Left *Lady Gaga arrives to perform the National Anthem as President-elect Joe Biden and Vice President-elect Kamala Harris watch during the 59th Presidential Inauguration, January 20, 2021, Washington, D.C.*

dove brooch and a flowing red silk faille skirt. Her operatic performance was bold and proud, and certainly wowed people who still thought she was "only" a pop star.

Gaga spent the late winter of 2020 and early spring of 2021 in Italy filming the Ridley Scott-helmed Gucci family biopic. Since she signed on to do the film, the cast had added a bevy of Hollywood superstars: Her co-lead was Adam Driver (*Girls*, *Star Wars*, *Marriage Story*), while other actors involved included Jared Leto, Jeremy Irons, Salma Hayek, and Al Pacino. "I wish to thank all of Italy for cheering me on while I film this movie—I hug and kiss you, tell you I believe in you," she tweeted in early May, before offering emojis of a red heart, the flag of Italy and folded hands. She added "prayers" to her "place of origin—a country built on the promise of hard work and family, I hope I made you proud. I'm proud to be Italian. Ti Amo."

Gaga returned to the spotlight in a big way several weeks later, when West Hollywood, California, christened May 23 as Born This Way Day, with a giant road mural that spelled out the phrase using the rainbow-hued designs of various pride flags. Gaga was on hand to celebrate in person, sporting a poofy updo, fishnets with giant holes and bright pink platform boots to accept a key to the city from Mayor Lindsey P. Horvath. "I'm sure this will sound cheesy to some people, not to me, but you've been the motherfucking key to my heart for a long time," Gaga said. "I'll honor this, I'll cherish this and I promise that I'll always be here for this day."

Her reverence and emotion was genuine. On Instagram, a clearly touched Gaga made sure to bring up the activist Carl Bean who had inspired "Born This Way," writing in an Instagram post, "Thank you for decades of relentless love, bravery, and a reason to sing. So we can all feel joy, because we deserve joy. Because we deserve the right to inspire tolerance, acceptance, and freedom for all."

This celebration was a much needed bright spot. In February, her dog walker, Ryan Fischer, was shot as he was walking her French bulldogs, Koji and Gustav, who were then stolen. Gaga offered a $500,000 reward for the dogs' return, writing on social media, "My heart is sick and I am praying my

family will be whole again with an act of kindness." Luckily, Fischer recovered, and Koji and Gustav were returned safely—five people were arrested in connection with the crime. In June, Gaga also postponed her Chromatica Ball dates *again*, to summer 2022, due to safety concerns around the ongoing COVID-19 pandemic.

As per usual, however, Gaga had things up her sleeve to assuage fan disappointment. She popped up during the much-anticipated reunion special for the nineties sitcom *Friends* and sang a duet with actress Lisa Kudrow. Sporting a nineties-esque, oversized magenta-and-yellow sweater and a hairdo with tiny braids, she strummed a red acoustic guitar and belted out the show's outsider-folk classic "Smelly Cat" with aplomb. In June, she also had a conversation with Dr. Bernice King, the CEO of The Martin Luther King Jr. Center for Nonviolent Social Change, about the "power of unlearning" and ways to dismantle white supremacy.

A few weeks later arrived a momentous date in the Gaga-verse: the tenth anniversary of *Born This Way*. It's charming to read her hopes for the album's endurance back in 2011, as she almost underestimated its staying power. "This new album is my chance to create what in 20 years will be seen as my iconic moment," she said at the time during a SHOWstudio.com interview. "That's what you should always aim at." Little did she know that just ten years later, fans and critics alike feted *Born This*

Above *As Patrizia Reggiani in Ridley Scott's* House of Gucci

Way as a culturally significant album. *Buzzfeed* ran a piece, "Here's How Lady Gaga's *Born This Way* Album Has Saved Lives For The Past Decade," rounding up rather moving remembrances from fans about the record's impact, such as "It captured the essence of the queer experience for me" and "'The Edge of Glory' really helped me through the death of my grandpa, and it taught me to celebrate life." The publication *Paper*, meanwhile, ran multiple essays on the album's impact on fashion and culture.

Gaga herself celebrated the milestone release of *Born This Way* with a pride-geared Versace capsule collection and a deluxe album reissue featuring a bonus covers EP, *Born This Way Reimagined: The Tenth Anniversary*. In a nod to the record's stature within the LGBTQIA+ community, she chose artists and allies for remakes: New Orleans bounce legend Big Freedia ("Judas"), pop superstar Kylie Minogue ("Marry the Night") and electro phenom Years & Years ("The Edge of Glory"). Nu-country star Orville Peck cut a new and soulful version of "Born This Way (The Country Road Version)," which was a bonus track on the original release, while Americana superstars The Highwomen, Brittney Spencer, and Madeline Edwards put a rootsy spin on "Highway Unicorn (Road To Love)." And, in a brilliant collaboration choice, Broadway star Ben Platt, who won a Tony Award for *Dear Evan Hansen*, contributed a stirring vocal take on "Yoü and I."

It was clear this EP was as much a gift to Gaga as it was to fans. "Thank you to each of the incredible artists who reimagined #BornThisWay songs!" she tweeted in celebration. "And thank you, Little Monsters, for building our community of love, acceptance, and kindness for the last 10 years. I'm so grateful for each of you. Rejoice and love yourself today 'cause baby, you were Born This Way."

And in late July, the highly anticipated *House of Gucci* trailer dropped. As a languid remix of Blondie's "Heart of Glass" trills in the background, Gaga showed off some of her high fashion looks she embraced, as well as some one liners—"It's time to take out the trash," "I don't consider myself to be a particularly ethical person, but I am fair"—that illustrated her character's conniving personality. The trailer drummed up excitement for the film—and positioned Gaga as a glam movie star. When *House of Gucci* opened in November, Gaga drew raves for her performance. One critic called it "Oscar-worthy," while others praised her acting, with one reviewer saying she was "never less than fascinating to watch." That wasn't the only positive news: Despite the up-and-down nature of the pandemic, she and Polansky weathered these tough times and were still going strong in August 2021. "Michael is her North Star," a source told *Entertainment Tonight*, adding that, "He is such a grounding and guiding presence for her." Perhaps even more important, the source noted that, "He loves Lady Gaga, but he's in love with Stefani."

Gaga makes balancing movie and music careers look easy; in hindsight, it's easy to see how she could've pursued acting instead. However, we're lucky she chose songwriting and performing, as the modern pop world would be completely different had Gaga not become a success. She not only brought weirdness back into the

Above *At the UK premiere of* House of Gucci*, November 9, 2021*

Right *Lady Gaga declares Born This Way Day as she reclines on a painted crosswalk on Robertson Boulevard in West Hollywood, California, on May 23, 2021*

mainstream, she built bridges between scenes and genres: New York downtown punk cool, sophisticated club culture, ecstatic dance floor electro, grimy dive-bar rock, arena-epic classic rock. Gaga taught multiple generations of fans and artists to be themselves and embrace their oddball quirks—and set high standards for pop stars to come: Katy Perry, Demi Lovato, Miley Cyrus, Ellie Goulding, Ariana Grande, Charli XCX, Tove Lo, Doja Cat, Dua Lipa, Olivia Rodrigo, and Willow Smith.

"For her it was very important to create a space and community to include everybody," her fashion director Nicola Formichetti told *Paper*. "And that's what was amazing for me, was seeing the beauty of pop culture where it's not too exclusive. It's very inclusive and community-based, and I feel like that's when this idea of the Little Monsters and her fandom really formed into this big community. It was very beautiful to see."

Gaga herself has grown and evolved during her time in the spotlight. The scrappy resilience she displayed early on in her career has blossomed into something more enduring—a steely resolve of personal strength and emotional generosity. "Whenever someone told me I wasn't good enough throughout my career and life, I never let it break me," she told *Vogue* in October 2020. "I promised myself that every time I heard 'no,' it would motivate me to work harder."

If you look through her interviews over time, this sentiment—using negativity and setbacks as motivation to do better and be more successful—was a common one. "Left hook, right hook," she told *Rolling Stone* in 2011. "I've been through so much worse in my life before I became a pop singer that I can feel no pain in the journey of the fight to the top." After referencing AC/DC's classic rock anthem, "It's a Long Way to the Top (If You Wanna Rock 'n' Roll)", she added "But at the end of the day, everything has a heart, everything has a soul—sometimes we forget that."

"Whenever someone told me I wasn't good enough throughout my career and life, I never let it break me. I promised myself that every time I heard 'no,' it would motivate me to work harder." LADY GAGA

Discography

THE FAME (2008)

Track List (US standard edition):

1. Just Dance (featuring Colby O'Donis)
2. LoveGame
3. Paparazzi
4. Poker Face
5. Eh, Eh (Nothing Else I Can Say)
6. Beautiful, Dirty, Rich
7. The Fame
8. Money Honey
9. Starstruck (featuring Space Cowboy and Flo Rida)
10. Boys Boys Boys
11. Paper Gangsta
12. Brown Eyes
13. I Like It Rough
14. Summerboy

Recorded

150 (Parsippany-Troy Hills, NJ); 333 (New York City, NY); Chalice (Los Angeles, CA); Cherrytree (Santa Monica, CA); Dojo (New York City, NY); Poe Boy (Miami, FL); Record Plant (Los Angeles, CA)

Released

October 28, 2008 (US), January 12, 2009 (UK)

Label

Streamline/KonLive/Cherrytree/Interscope

Songwriting

All songs co-written by Lady Gaga; other songwriters include Aliaune Thiam (Akon) (track 1); Brian Kierulf & Josh Schwartz (Brian & Josh) (track 14); Tramar Dillard (Flo Rida) (track 9); Rob Fusari (tracks 3, 6, 12); Bilal Hajji (track 8); Martin Kierszenbaum (tracks 5, 7, 9, 13); Nadir Khayat (RedOne) (tracks 1, 2, 4, 8, 10, 11); Nik Dresti (Space Cowboy) (track 9)

Production

Lady Gaga (tracks 3, 12); Brian & Josh (track 14); Rob Fusari (tracks 3, 6, 12); Martin Kierszenbaum (tracks 5, 7, 9, 13); RedOne (tracks 1, 2, 4, 8, 10, 11); Space Cowboy (track 9)

Notable Personnel

Rapper Flo Rida appears on "Starstruck."

Highest chart position on release

1 (Canada, Ireland, Germany, UK), 2 (Czech Republic, France, New Zealand, US), 3 (Australia, Spain), 5 (Russia), 6 (Japan), 13 (Italy), 15 (Sweden)

Notes

The Fame had different release dates in various territories throughout 2008 and 2009. Many of these versions also had different bonus tracks, depending on the country of release. For example, the Japanese editions had the disco-rock anthem "Retro Dance Freak," while "Disco Heaven" was a bonus track on the UK standard version.

THE FAME MONSTER (2009)

Track List
1. Bad Romance
2. Alejandro
3. Monster
4. Speechless
5. Dance In The Dark
6. Telephone
7. So Happy I Could Die
8. Teeth

Recorded
Darkchild Studios (Los Angeles, CA); FC Walvisch (Amsterdam, Netherlands); Metropolis Studios (London, UK); Record Plant (Los Angeles, CA); Studio Groove (Osaka, Japan)

Released
November 23, 2009 (US & UK)

Label
Streamline/KonLive/Cherrytree/Interscope

Songwriting
All songs written or co-written by Lady Gaga; other songwriters include Beyoncé (track 6); LaShawn Daniels (track 6); Lazonate Franklin (track 6); Fernando Garibay (track 5); Rodney "Darkchild" Jerkins (track 6); RedOne (tracks 1, 2, 3, 7); Taja Riley (track 8); Space Cowboy (tracks 3, 7)

Production
All songs co-produced by Lady Gaga; other producers include Ron Fair (track 4); Fernando Garibay (track 5); Tal Herzberg (track 4); Rodney "Darkchild" Jerkins (track 6); RedOne (tracks 1–3, 7); Teddy Riley (track 8); Space Cowboy (track 7)

Notable Personnel: Beyoncé co-wrote and features on "Telephone," while Grammy-winning Mark "Spike" Stent mixed "Bad Romance" and "Telephone"

Highest chart position on release
1 (Australia, New Zealand), 2 (Italy, Japan, Sweden), 3 (Czech Republic, Russia), 5 (US), 6 (Canada), 13 (France)

Notes
The Fame Monster was issued as an EP appended to *The Fame* but was also released in multiple different versions around the world in 2009 and 2010, including as a stand-alone release. For example, a super deluxe version included some hair from an actual Gaga wig, while a USB edition featured re-dos and remixes, such as "LoveGame (Robots to Mars Remix)."

Separately, in 2010 Gaga released a remix album combining songs from *The Fame* and *The Fame Monster* titled, simply, *The Remix*. Issued on May 4 in the UK and August 3 in the US, the full-length featured a Passion Pit remix of "Telephone" and Stuart Price re-do of "Paparazzi," as well as rocker Marilyn Manson appearing on a growling remix of "LoveGame." *The Remix* peaked at No. 3 in the UK and No. 6 in the US.

BORN THIS WAY (2011)

Track List

1. Marry The Night
2. Born This Way
3. Government Hooker
4. Judas
5. Americano
6. Hair
7. Scheiße
8. Bloody Mary
9. Bad Kids
10. Highway Unicorn (Road To Love)
11. Heavy Metal Lover
12. Electric Chapel
13. Yoü And I
14. The Edge Of Glory

Recorded

Abbey Road Studios (London, UK); Allertown Hill (London, UK); Gang Studios (Paris, France); Germano Studios (New York, NY); Officine Mechaniche Studios (Milano, Italy); Paradise Studios (Birmingham, UK); Studio 301 (Sydney, Australia); Studio at the Palms (Las Vegas, NV); Studio Bus (mobile tour bus recording studio); The Living Room Studios (Oslo, Norway); The Mix Room (Burbank, CA); Warehouse Productions (Omaha, NE)

Released

May 23, 2011

Label

Streamline/KonLive/
Interscope Records

Songwriting

All songs written or co-written by Lady Gaga; other songwriters include Fernando Garibay (tracks 1–3, 5, 8–11, 14); Jeppe Laursen (tracks 2, 9); Brian Lee (tracks 5, 10); RedOne (tracks 4, 6, 7); William Sami Étienne Grigahcine (DJ Snake) (track 3); Clinton Sparks (tracks 3, 8); Paul Edward Blair (DJ White Shadow) (tracks 2, 3, 5, 8–10, 12, 14)

Production

Songs 1–13 co-produced by Lady Gaga; other producers include Fernando Garibay (tracks 1, 2, 5, 9–11, 14); Robert John "Mutt" Lange (track 13); Jeppe Laursen (tracks 2, 9); RedOne (tracks 4, 6, 7, 10); DJ White Shadow (tracks 2, 3, 5, 8, 9, 10, 12)

Notable Personnel

E Street Band saxophonist Clarence Clemons appeared on "The Edge Of Glory" and Queen guitarist Brian May was on "Yoü And I."

Highest chart position on release

1 (Australia, Canada, Czech Republic, France, Germany, Ireland, Italy, Japan, New Zealand, Russia, Sweden, UK, US), 2 (Spain)

Notes

The album sold an incredible 1.1 million copies in its first week on sale in the US. Globally, there were also different versions of *Born This Way* released, including one featuring the bonus track "Black Jesus + Amen Fashion." On November 21, 2011, Gaga released her second remix album, *Born This Way: The Remix*, in the US and UK. The full-length featured remixes of songs by Goldfrapp, The Weeknd, Zedd, and Twin Shadow, among others. *Born This Way: The Remix* peaked at No. 77 in the UK and No. 105 in the US.

ARTPOP (2013)

Track List

1. Aura
2. Venus
3. G.U.Y.
4. Sexxx Dreams
5. Jewels N' Drugs *(featuring T.I., Too $hort and Twista)*
6. MANiCURE
7. Do What U Want *(featuring R. Kelly)*
8. ARTPOP
9. Swine
10. Donatella
11. Fashion!
12. Mary Jane Holland
13. Dope
14. Gypsy
15. Applause

Recorded

80 Hertz Studios (Manchester, UK); CRC Studios (Chicago, IL); Patchwerk Studios (Atlanta, GA); Piano Music Studios (Amsterdam, NL); Platinum Sound Recording Studios (New York City, NY); Record Plant (Los Angeles, CA); Shangri-La Studios (Malibu, CA)

Released

November 11, 2013

Label

Streamline/Interscope

Songwriting

All songs co-written by Lady Gaga; other songwriters include Julien Arias (track 15); David Guetta (track 11); Clifford Harris Jr. (T.I.) (track 5); Amit Duvdevani and Erez Eisen (Infected Mushroom) (track 1); R. Kelly (track 7); Hugo Pierre Leclercq (Madeon) (tracks 2, 12, 14); Nicolas Mercier (track 15); Carl Mitchell (track 5); Nick Monson (tracks 2, 5, 6, 8, 9, 13, 15); RedOne (track 14); Todd Shaw (track 5); DJ Snake (tracks 4, 7, 15); Sun Ra (track 2); Martin Bresso (Tchami) (tracks 4, 7, 15); Giorgio Tuinfort (track 11); DJ White Shadow (tracks 2, 4–9, 11, 13-15); will.i.am (track 11); Anton Zaslavski (Zedd) (tracks 1, 3, 10); Dino Zisis (tracks 2, 5, 6, 8, 9, 13, 15)

Production

All songs produced or co-produced by Lady Gaga; other producers include David Guetta (track 11); Infected Mushroom (track 1); Madeon (tracks 12, 14); Nick Monson (tracks 5, 6, 8, 9, 15); Rick Rubin (track 13); Giorgio Tuinfort (track 11); DJ White Shadow (tracks 4–9, 15); will.i.am (track 11); Zedd (tracks 1, 3, 10); Dino Zisis (tracks 5, 6, 8, 9, 15)

Notable Personnel

Rappers T.I., Twista, Too $hort, and R. Kelly appear, as does Rick Rubin. One-time Whitesnake and Dio guitarist Doug Aldrich plays on "MANiCURE," while guitarist Tim Stewart, who has played with Infectious Grooves, also contributes to several songs.

Highest chart position on release

1 (Japan, US, UK), 2 (Australia, Ireland, Italy, New Zealand), 3 (Canada, Czech Republic, France, Germany, Spain), 6 (Sweden)

Notes

Sun Ra has a writing credit on *ARTPOP* because the song "Venus" samples a cover of "Rocket Number 9" done by a French electropop group called Zombie Zombie.

CHEEK TO CHEEK
(WITH TONY BENNETT) (2014)

Track List

1. Anything Goes
2. Cheek To Cheek
3. Nature Boy
4. I Can't Give You Anything But Love
5. I Won't Dance
6. Firefly
7. Lush Life
8. Sophisticated Lady
9. Let's Face The Music And Dance
10. But Beautiful
11. It Don't Mean A Thing (If It Ain't Got That Swing)

Recorded

Avatar Studio C (New York, NY); Kaufman Astoria Studios (Astoria, New York, NY); Manhattan Centre Studios (New York, NY)

Released

September 22, 2014 (UK); September 23, 2014 (US)

Label

Columbia/Streamline/Interscope

Songwriting

eden ahbez (track 3); Irving Berlin (tracks 2, 9); Johnny Burke (track 10); Cy Coleman (track 6); Duke Ellington (tracks 8, 11); Dorothy Fields (tracks 4, 5); Oscar Hammerstein II (track 5); Otto Harbach (track 5); Jerome Kern (track 5); Carolyn Leigh (track 6); Jimmy McHugh (tracks 4, 5); Irving Mills (tracks 8, 11); Mitchell Parish (track 8); Cole Porter (track 1); Billy Strayhorn (track 7); Jimmy Van Heusen (track 10)

Production

All tracks produced by Dae Bennett.

Notable Personnel

The album is a collaboration with the legendary crooner Tony Bennett. Bennett and Gaga used a variety of session jazz musicians, including members of Bennett's band, for the recording.

Highest chart position on release

1 (Sweden [Jazz], US), 3 (Canada, New Zealand), 4 (Czech Republic), 5 (Spain), 6 (Italy), 7 (Australia, Japan), 9 (France), 10 (UK), 12 (Germany, Ireland)

Notes

With this album, Lady Gaga became the first female solo artist to have three No. 1 US albums in the 2010s. Tony Bennett also extended his record as the oldest artist to have a No. 1 album.

JOANNE (2016)

Track List

1. Diamond Heart
2. A-YO
3. Joanne
4. John Wayne
5. Dancin' In Circles
6. Perfect Illusion
7. Million Reasons
8. Sinner's Prayer
9. Come To Mama
10. Hey Girl *(featuring Florence Welch)*
11. Angel Down

Recorded

123 Studios (London, UK); Diamond Mine Recording Co. (New York City, NY); Dragonfly Recording Studios (Malibu, CA); Electric Lady Studios (New York City, NY); The Farm (London, UK); GenPop Laboratory (Los Angeles, CA); Green Oak Studios (Los Angeles, CA); Gypsy Palace (Malibu, CA); Pink Duck Studios (Burbank, CA); Shangri-La Studios (Malibu, CA); Vox Recording Studios (Los Angeles, CA); Zelig (London, England)

Released

October 21, 2016

Label

Streamline/Interscope

Songwriting

All songs co-written by Lady Gaga; other songwriters include Michael Tucker (BloodPop) (tracks 2, 4–6); Thomas Brenneck (track 8); Beck Hansen (track 5); Emile Haynie (track 9); Josh Homme (tracks 1, 4); Hillary Lindsey (tracks 2, 7); Kevin Parker (track 6); RedOne (track 11); Mark Ronson (tracks 1–8, 10); Josh Tillman (tracks 8, 9); Florence Welch (track 10)

Production

All songs co-produced by Lady Gaga, Mark Ronson, and BloodPop; other producers include Jeff Bhasker (track 1); Emile Haynie (track 9); Josh Homme (track 1); Kevin Parker (track 6)

Notable Personnel

Florence Welch sings on and co-wrote "Hey Girl," while the album also features contributions from Josh Homme, Beck Hansen and Tame Impala's Kevin Parker.

Highest chart position on release

1 (Japan, US), 2 (Australia, Canada, Italy, New Zealand, Spain), 3 (Czech Republic, Ireland, Sweden, UK), 6 (Germany), 9 (France)

Notes

Joanne was a departure for Gaga, as the album toned down the dance-oriented electronic flourishes in favor of more personal, introspective songwriting. The death of Gaga's aunt Joanne Stefani Germanotta deeply influenced the album.

A STAR IS BORN SOUNDTRACK (2018)

Track List

1. Black Eyes
2. La Vie En Rose
3. Maybe It's Time
4. Out Of Time
5. Alibi
6. Shallow
7. Music To My Eyes
8. Diggin' My Grave
9. Always Remember Us This Way
10. Look What I Found
11. Heal Me
12. I Don't Know What Love Is
13. Is That Alright?
14. Why Did You Do That?
15. Hair Body Face
16. Before I Cry
17. Too Far Gone
18. I'll Never Love Again *(Film Version)*
19. I'll Never Love Again *(Extended Version)*

Recorded

EastWest Studios (Los Angeles, CA); Electric Lady Studios (New York City, NY); Shangri-La Studios (Malibu, CA); The Village West (Los Angeles, CA); Woodrow Wilson Studios (Hollywood, CA)

Released

October 5, 2018

Label

Interscope

Songwriting

Lady Gaga co-wrote tracks 5–7, 9–16, 18, 19; other songwriters include Bradley Cooper (tracks 1, 4, 5, 17); Natalie Hemby (track 9, 18, 19); Jason Isbell (track 3); Paul Kennerley (track 8); Hillary Lindsey (track 9, 18, 19); Louiguy (track 2); Lori McKenna (track 9); Julia Michaels (track 11); Nick Monson (tracks 10, 11, 13–16); Lukas Nelson (tracks 1, 4, 5, 7, 10, 12, 13, 17); Mark Nilan Jr. (tracks 10, 11, 13–16); Édith Piaf (track 2); Aaron Raitiere (tracks 10, 13 ,18, 19); Mark Ronson (track 6); Anthony Rossomando (track 6); Justin Tranter (track 11); Diane Warren (track 14); DJ White Shadow (tracks 10, 11, 13–16); Andrew Wyatt (track 6)

Production

Lady Gaga co-produced songs 1-3, 5, 6, 8-16, 18, 19; other producers include Dave Cobb (track 9); Bradley Cooper (tracks 1, 3, 4, 5, 17); Nick Monson (tracks 10–16); Lukas Nelson (tracks 1, 4, 5, 7, 8, 12, 17); Brian Newman (track 2); Mark Nilan Jr. (tracks 10–16); Benjamin Rice (tracks 3, 6, 15, 18, 19); and DJ White Shadow (tracks 10, 11, 13–16)

Notable Personnel

Actor Bradlcy Cooper contributed songwriting, production and vocals, while Willie Nelson's son, Lukas Nelson, and Nashville producer Dave Cobb also contributed.

Highest chart position on release

1 (Australia, Canada, Czech Republic, Ireland, France, New Zealand, UK, US), 2 (Spain), 4 (Germany, Italy), 12 (Japan)

Notes

A *Star Is Born* came in a version with movie dialogue interspersed between songs, and a version with just the music. The soundtrack became Gaga's longest-running No. 1 album in the US, as the LP debuted at the top of the chart and spent three consecutive weeks at the peak, and later returned to the top spot for a fourth week. The A *Star Is Born* soundtrack also spent ten weeks atop the Australian album charts.

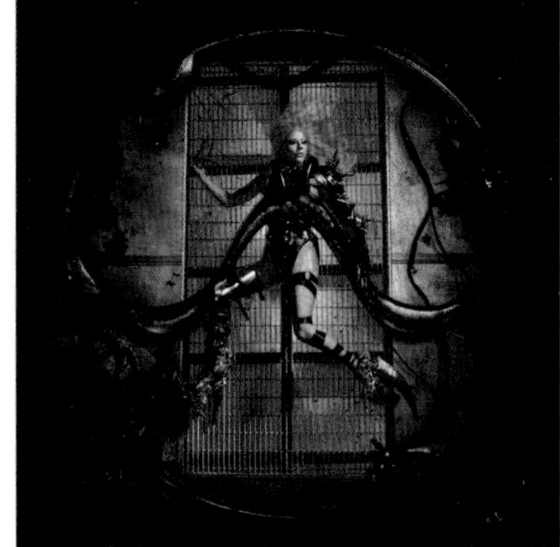

CHROMATICA (2020)

Track List

1. Chromatica I
2. Alice
3. Stupid Love
4. Rain On Me (*featuring Ariana Grande*)
5. Free Woman
6. Fun Tonight
7. Chromatica II
8. 911
9. Plastic Doll
10. Sour Candy (*featuring Blackpink*)
11. Enigma
12. Replay
13. Chromatica III
14. Sine From Above (*featuring Elton John*)
15. 1000 Doves
16. Babylon

Recorded

Conway Recording (Hollywood, CA); EastWest (Hollywood, CA); Electric Lady (New York City, NY); Sterling Sound (New York City, NY); Good Father (Los Angeles, CA); Henson Recording (Los Angeles, CA); MXM Studios (Los Angeles, CA); Utility Muffin Research Kitchen (Hollywood Hills, CA)

Released

May 29, 2020

Label

Streamline/Interscope

Songwriting

All songs co-written by Lady Gaga; other songwriters include Salem Al Fakir (track 14); Axel Christofer Hedfors (Axwell) (tracks 2, 5, 14); BloodPop (tracks 2–6, 8–12, 14–16); Alexander Ridha (Boys Noize) (track 4); Matthew Burns (tracks 4, 6, 10–12, 16); Nija Charles (track 4); Ariana Grande (track 4); Jacob "Jkash" Hindlin (tracks 9, 11); Sebastian Ingrosso (track 14); Elton John (track 14); Morgan Kibby (tracks 1, 7, 13); Johannes Klahr (tracks 2, 5, 14); Madison Love (track 10); Madeon (track 8); Max Martin (track 3); Teddy Park (track 10); Vincent Pontare (track 14); Benjamin Rice (track 14); Ely Rise (track 3); Sonny John Moore (Skrillex) (track 9); Tchami (tracks 3, 4, 15); Ryan Tedder (track 14); Justin Tranter (tracks 2, 8); Rami Yacoub (tracks 4, 6, 9, 10, 14, 15); Richard Zastenker (track 14)

Production

Lady Gaga co-produced songs 1, 7 and 13; other producers include Axwell (tracks 2, 5, 14); BloodPop (tracks 2–6, 8–11, 14–16); Burns (tracks 4, 6, 10–12, 14, 16); Morgan Kibby (tracks 1, 7, 13); Johannes Klahr (tracks 2, 5, 14); Liohn (track 14); Madeon (track 8); Max Martin (track 3); Benjamin Rice (tracks 2–6, 8–12, 14–16); Skrillex (track 9); Tchami (tracks 3, 4, 15, 16); Yacoub (track 14)

Notable Personnel

Elton John sings on and co-wrote "Sine From Above"; Ariana Grande sings on and co-wrote "Rain On Me"; Blackpink appears on "Sour Candy."

Highest chart position on release

1 (Australia, Canada, Czech Republic, France, Ireland, Italy, New Zealand, UK, US), 2 (Spain, Sweden), 3 (Germany, Japan)

Notes

Chromatica has additional bonus tracks for other territories, including alternate versions of "Stupid Love" and "1000 Doves." On September 3, 2021, Gaga released her third remix album, *Dawn of Chromatica*. The effort featured re-dos of *Chromatica* tunes by Charli XCX, Rina Sawayama, Planningtorock, and Shygirl and Mura Masa. *Dawn of Chromatica* peaked at No. 56 in the UK and No. 66 in the US.

LOVE FOR SALE
(WITH TONY BENNETT) (2021)

Track List
1. It's De-Lovely
2. Night And Day
3. Love For Sale
4. Do I Love You
5. I Concentrate On You
6. I Get A Kick Out Of You
7. So In Love
8. Let's Do It (Let's Fall In Love)
9. Just One Of Those Things
10. Dream Dancing

Recorded
Electric Lady Studios (New York City, NY)

Released
October 1, 2021 (worldwide)

Label
Streamline/Columbia/Interscope

Songwriting
All songs written by Cole Porter

Production
Dae Bennett

Notable Personnel
Grammy award-winning composer Jorge Calandrelli arranged and conducted the orchestra. Dae Bennett, who produced the album, is Tony Bennett's son. His son, Danny Bennett also contributed, as did his daughter, and Tony's grand-daughter Kelsey Bennett, who oversaw photography.

Highest chart position on release
1 (Australia [Jazz], France [Jazz], Sweden [Jazz] US [Jazz]), 5 (Germany), 6 (France, UK), 8 (Italy, US)

Notes
Bennett's final album before retirement. He sings two solo songs, "So In Love" and "Just One Of Those Things," while Gaga solos on "Do I Love You" and "Let's Do It (Let's Fall In Love)." The release of *Love For Sale* saw Bennett break the Guinness World Record for the oldest person to release an album of new material, at the age of ninety-five years and sixty days.

Acknowledgments

T: Top; **B:** Bottom; **L:** Left; **R:** Right
ALAMY: COVER: PictureLux /The Hollywood Archive/Alamy Stock Photo **P17T** f8 archive/Alamy Stock Photo **P17BR** EyeBrowz/Alamy Stock Photo **P17BL** sjvinyl/Alamy Stock Photo **P24-25** Chaz Niell/Southcreek EMI/ZUMA Press **P30** Wendy Connett/Alamy Stock Photo **P35, P180** Pictorial Press Ltd/Alamy Stock Photo **P49, P86, P86-87, P116, P130-131, P134, P165TR** WENN Rights Ltd/Alamy Stock Photo **P64T** NBC-TV/Album **P76-77** Album/Alamy Stock Photo **P79** The Photo Access/Alamy Stock Photo **P97** Abaca Press/Alamy Stock Photo **P100** ABC/Album **P101** Olivier Douliery/ABACAPRESS.COM **P105-105, P107** Imaginechina Limited/Alamy Stock Photo **P118-119** REUTERS/Toru Hana **P120** REUTERS/Lucas Jackson **P142-143** BBC/Album **P144** Marco Piraccini/Mondadori Portfolio/Sipa USA **P147** Derek Storm/Everett Collection/Alamy Live News **P171** Sipa US/Alamy Stock Photo **P175** Doug Peters/Alamy Stock Photo **P178** APL Archive/Alamy Stock Photo **P181** LANDMARK MEDIA/Alamy Stock Photo **P182** Collection Christophel/Alamy Stock Photo **P183T** Photo 12/Alamy Stock Photo **P203** Luke Durda/Alamy Stock Photo **P205** REUTERS/Marco Bello **P210-211** dpa picture alliance/Alamy Live News **P212** Metro-Goldwyn-Mayer (MGM)/Album/Alamy Stock Photo **www.flickr.com: P28** atp_tyreseus **GETTY: P6** Gareth Cattermole/Getty Images **P8, P89, P108T, P186, P201, P204** (for MTV) Kevin Winter/Getty Images **P9B** Patrick Beaudry/Getty Images **P11, P19, P40-41, P62, P66, P108B, P110-111** (for Born This Way Foundation), **P122-123** (for MTV), **P128, P132, P138, P150-151, P168** Kevin Mazur/WireImage **P12-13** ANDREAS BRANCH/Patrick McMullan via Getty Images **P14, P141** Chelsea Lauren/WireImage **P16** Larry Busacca/Getty Images for Giorgio Armani **P18, P33** Jason Squires/WireImage **P20** Chris Gabrin/Redferns **P21** Paul Bergen/Redferns **P26, P155, P192-193** (for AT&T) Theo Wargo/WireImage **P29** Eric CATARINA/Gamma-Rapho via Getty Images **P31** David Corio/Michael Ochs Archives/Getty Images **P34** Michael Putland/Getty Images **P36L, P38-39** Roger Kisby/Getty Images **P36R** Eugene Gologursky/WireImage **P37, P78, P124** (for 42 West), **P126** D. Kambouris/WireImage **P42** Jeff Fusco/Getty Images **P46** Ross Marino/Getty Images **P47** Weegee(Arthur Fellig)/International Center of Photography/Getty Images **P48** John Medina/WireImage **P50-51** Bennett Raglin/WireImage **P52-53, P67** Dave M. Benett/Getty Images **P54** Jakubaszek/Getty Images **P55** Daniel Boczarski/Redferns **P56-57** George Pimentel/WireImage **P60, P117** (for Children Mending Hearts), Christopher Polk/Getty Images **P63** LEON NEAL/AFP via Getty Images **P72-73** Michael Caulfield/WireImage **P74** The Sydney Morning Herald/Fairfax Media via Getty Images via Getty Images **P80** Jason Merritt/Getty Images **P81** Ollie Millington/Redferns **P82-83** Neil Lupin/Redferns **P90-91** ALBERTO PIZZOLI/AFP via Getty Images **P92** Hamid Mousa-Cool Kids Club/Getty Images **P94** Tim Greenway/Portland Press Herald via Getty Images **P98** Gie Knaeps/Getty Images **P102-103** Anthony Harvey/Getty Images **P106** Visual China Group via Getty Images **P112** Paul Morigi/WireImage **P127** Gary Gershoff/WireImage **P133, P148, P149** (for Citi) **P152, P153** (for RPM) **P166-167, P172** (for Live Nation) **P194, P196, P197, P198, P199** (for Park MGM Las Vegas) **P200** (for Haus Laboratories) **P214** (for LG) Kevin Mazur/Getty Images **P135, P136-137** Christopher Polk/WireImage **P146** Jeff Kravitz/WireImage **P156-157, P174B** Jun Sato/WireImage **P158** Francis Specker/CBS via Getty Images **P160-161** MARK RALSTON/AFP via Getty Images **P162** James Keivom/New York Daily News **P163** James Devaney/WireImage **P165TL** Ray Tamarra/GC Images **P165BR** James Devaney/GC Images **P169, P170** Patrick Smith/Getty Images **P173** Scott Legato/Getty Images for Live Nation **P174T** David Becker/Getty Images **P176-177** FILIPPO MONTEFORTE/AFP via Getty Images **P187** ROBYN BECK/AFP via Getty Images **P188-189** Matt Petit-Handout/A.M.P.A.S. via Getty Images **P202** Jason Koerner/Getty Images for Oprah **P206-207** Raymond Hall/GC Images **P208** Dimitrios Kambouris/Getty Images for National Board of Review **P213** Samir Hussein/WireImage **REX SHUTTERSTOCK: P4** Christopher Polk/Shutterstock **P9T** Invision/AP/Shutterstock **P22-23** Ronald Wittek/EPA/Shutterstock **P44** Erik Pendzich/Shutterstock **P59** Brendan Beirne/Shutterstock **P64B** Ken McKay/ITV/Shutterstock **P68-69** Nam Y Huh/AP/Shutterstock **P70** Paul Grover/Shutterstock **P88** BDG/Shutterstock **P109** Matt Sayles/AP/Shutterstock **P114** Al Pastor/Shutterstock **P129** Lincoln Square Prods/Sunset Lane/Kobal/Shutterstock **P154** Gregory Pace/BEI/Shutterstock **P165BL** Buzz Foto/Shutterstock **P183B** Prashant Gupta/Fx/Kobal/Shutterstock **P184-185** Warner Bros/Kobal/Shutterstock **P190** David Fisher/Shutterstock

ALBUM COVERS: P215 Pieter Henket, Candice Lawler, Warwick Saint (photography), Liam Ward (design) **P216** Julian Peploe Studio (art direction) Hedi Slimane (photography) **P217** Nick Knight (creation, photography) Nicola Formichetti, Laurieann Gibson, Todd Tourso (creation) **P218** Jeff Koons (album cover, package design) **P219** Ianthe Zevos (creative director), Steven Klein (photographer) **P220** Andrea Gelardin, Ruth Hogben, Lady Gaga (creative direction, photography) Brandon Maxwell (creative direction, fashion direction) Brian Roettinger, An Yen (graphic design) Collier Schorr, Florence Welch (photography) **P221** Peter Lindbergh, Clay Enos (photography) Concept Arts, Inc. (album design) **P222** Norbert Schoerner, Brandon Bowen (photography) Nicola Formichetti (fashion direction) Bryan Rivera, Isha Dipika Walia, Travis Brothers (creative direction, design) Aditya Pamidi (art manager) **P223** Kelsey Bennett (photography) Ted Lovett (art direction) Patrick Waugh (Collage Artist)

Sources

www.aarp.org; www.abcnews.go.com; www.apnews.com; www.bbc.com; www.billboard.com; www.bornthisway.foundation; www.buzzfeed.com; www.capradio.org; www.cbsnews.com; www.completemusicupdate.com; www.dailymail.co.uk; www.dailystar.co.uk; www.eonline.com; www.elle.com; www.ew.com; www.factmag.com; www.findagrave.com; www.forbes.com; www.harpersbazaar.com; www.herworld.com; www.hollywoodreporter.com; www.huffpost.com; www.ibtimes.com; www.independent.co.uk; www.independent.ie; www.insider.com; www.instyle.com; www.ladygaga.fandom.com; www.lamaisongaga.com; www.metacritic.com; www.mtv.com; www.music-news.com; www.nbcbayarea.com; www.newspapers.com; www.newsweek.com; www.nme.com; www.nycago.org; www.nydailynews.com; www.nymag.com; www.nypost.com; www.nytimes.com; www.nyuirhc.org; www.observer.com; www.out.com; www.papermag.com; www.people.com; www.popcrush.com; www.pri.org; www.racked.com; www.rollingstone.com; www.scifivision.com; www.today.com; www.thedailybeast.com; www.thefader.com; www.theguardian.com; www.time.com; www.twitter.com; www.undergroundfairy.blogspot.com; www.usmagazine.com; www.usatoday.com; www.variety.com; www.versace.com; www.vice.com; www.vogue.com; www.web.archive.org; www.en.wikipedia.org; www.wkyc.com; www.wwd.com; www.youtube.com; www.yahoo.com